D1831818

GANDHIAN THOUGHTS

GANDHIAN THOUGHTS
An Overview

Dr. Ravindra Kumar

GYAN PUBLISHING HOUSE
NEW DELHI-110002

Gandhian Thoughts : An Overview

ISBN: 81-212-0914-5

Rs. 360

© Dr. Ravindra Kumar

All rights reserved. No part of this book may be reproduced in any manner without written permission.

Published in 2006 in India by
Gyan Publishing House
5, Ansari Road, Daryaganj, New Delhi-110002
Phones : 23261060, 23282060, Fax : 91-011-23282060
E-mail : books@gyanbooks.com
Website : http://www.gyanbooks.com

Laser Typesetting at: Master Computers, Delhi
Printed at: Salasar Imaging System, Delhi

Dedicated to

Prof. Dr. Preedee Kasemsup

CONTENTS

FOREWORD

I am glad to learn that Dr. Ravindra Kumar's latest work titled *Gandhian Thoughts: An Overview* is to be released soon.

The relevance and importance of Gandhian Thoughts, which revalue around Ahimsa, an all timely value and an active force essential for existence and development, can never be underrated.

If we want to get rid of problems and want a peaceful life based on co-existence, it is a categorical imperative to adopt Gandhian approach and to put it in day-to-day practices individually and collectively at different levels.

Dr. Ravindra Kumar is among the few distinguished scholars who keep the flag of Gandhism flying high even today when corruption, criminalization, caste and community-based vote bank politics and competitive consumerism have become the main stream of our national life.

My best wishes for the success of Dr. Ravindra Kumar's book.

Subhash C Kashyap

INTRODUCTION

To think about general people and to work for them selflessly was the prime objective of the life of Mahatma Gandhi. That is why, Gandhism discusses day-to-day problems which a human being faces, and suggests their remedial solutions. Perhaps, not a single human problem remained untouched, for which Mahatma Gandhi had not expressed his views and on the basis of his experiences of life, had not suggested the way to get rid of it.

Not only before the people of India but also of all nations of the world, whether poor, developing or developed, the rise of problems in one form or other is natural. In other words, people of not a single country are free from the problems; they cannot get rid of them completely. However, if efforts are made in the right direction then definitely relief can be attained to a great extent from both types of problems- internal and external.

The way shown by Mahatma Gandhi to get rid of the day-to-day problems whether they are big or small; of local, national or international level was very effective in his time. That is why; Indians were capable to solve their problem pertaining to independence and after independence were able to march on the path of progress.

Still Indians have to resolve many problems. They have to work for a India in which, according to Mahatma Gandhi, *"there shall be no high class and low class of people; in which all communities shall live in perfect harmony. There can be no room in such an India for the curse of untouchability or the curse of the intoxicating drinks and drugs. Women will enjoy the same rights as men. Indians shall be at peace with the rest of the world, neither exploiting, nor being exploited, they should have the smallest army imaginable."*

Furthermore the whole world has to establish the true environment in which each and everyone should get peace and prosperity. No doubt, to fulfill this dream the path shown by Mahatma Gandhi is like a ray of hope before all. The direction given by him is more important and effective today than it was in his own times.

After my retirement in 1994 from the post of Vice Chancellor of Meerut University, I got several opportunities to write on different aspects of Gandhian philosophy for various universities and institutions in India and abroad and on the basis of them the preparation of this manuscript could be possible. I hope that after publication this book will be useful to general readers and all those interested in Mahatma Gandhi and his social, political, educational, economic and cultural thoughts.

I am thankful to Mr. V. B. Pant, Mr. Sachin Bathala, Mr. Manoj Kumar 'Manoj', Mrs. Manju Singh and Mrs. Megha for their help and active support, which they have extended in preparation of this manuscript.

Ravindra Kumar

23-B, Lane : 2
Mansarovar, Civil Lines,
MEERUT-250 001 [India]
Phone: 0121-2640549
E-mail: ravindrakumar5@ hotmail.com
ravindrakumar5@rediffmail.com

ABBREVIATIONS

A. D.	:	After the death of Christ
B. C.	:	Before Christ
I. P. R. A.	:	International Peace Research Association
M. B. A.	:	Master of Business Administration
P. E. C.	:	Peace Education Commission
R. G. P. G.	:	Raghunath Girls Post Graduate College [at Meerut]
U. N. O.	:	United Nations Organizations
U. S. A.	:	United States of America
U. S. S. R.	:	Union of Soviet Socialist Republic

"Generations to come... will scarcely believe that such a one as this even in flesh and blood walked upon this earth."

–(Albert Einstein)

CHAPTER–1

GANDHI AND RELIGION

It is a celebrated fact that Mahatma Gandhi always believed in the omnipotent, omniscient, omnipresent Almighty God that, according to him, demands self-surrender.[1] This faith is fully based on the everlasting practices of *Vedic*-Hindu philosophy. For Mahatma Gandhi God is the ultimate limit of truth, and the ultimate power which governs the activities of the world. He always believed in the power of God. He also believed that the logic is almost significant in comparison to His sovereignty. In this context, his religious point of view was shaped by the expression of life also. To comprehend his religious belief, we should know about those factors that laid the foundation stone of his faith.

1. HINDU SANATAN DHARMA

By birth Mahatma Gandhi was a Hindu *Sanatanist*; he inherited his convictions from his religious community and ancestors. He never gave them up. Among these, the first is faith in God, the second is of God and Truth, and then is *Ahinsa*-the non-violence, celibacy and collectivism. Mahatma Gandhi accepted God, truth and non-violence as one. Hinduism lays emphasis on the omnipresence of God, and this is what he believes. There is absolutely no place for any logic, because a follower of truth experiences it at every step. He wrote in this context in Young India on 11 October 1928:

"*It is implicit, mysterious all pervading power which cannot be seen with eyes but can be felt with the heart. This power cannot be dealt with logically but can definitely be experienced by senses.*"

It has been stated in the *Upanishad* that truth, knowledge and the Creator are one. Therefore, Mahatma Gandhi used to say that truth is God or "*Truth is my behaviour in my God.*" He believed that God is truth and anything, which is true, is God. Truth is what is essential.

Non-violence is the best religion. In *Mahabharata* it is acknowledged, "*Non-violence is the supreme religion.*" Mahatma Gandhi accepted it as his religion under its influence. Later on he elaborated and analyzed it in his own way. The word non-violence is negative but in its meaning it is positive. As a word its meaning is not to hurt anyone through words or actions-*Mansa-vacha-karmana*. It states love for everyone. Briefly, these convictions were the source of Mahatma Gandhi's religion and gave birth to *Satyagraha*.

Celibacy, or purity of sex, increases the spiritual energy. One should indulge in sex not for pleasure but for procreation. One should not believe in acquisitiveness or hoarding money. One should enjoy life according to one's nature guided by the ancient *Varna* system. His belief that one should be likewise and thus be generous was also inspired by the principles of Hinduism.

BUDDHISM AND JAINISM

As a true Hindu, Mahatma Gandhi acknowledged the greatness of Gautama-the Buddha and said :

"*Buddha had adopted all that is best in Hinduism. He spent his life discovering the precepts that were implicit in the Vedas.*[2] *Although he did not believe in Altruism of God but he rejected the evil practice of those who consider themselves to be custodians of God.*[3] *He repeatedly and strongly emphasized that the moral principle of the world is unchanging and permanent, and unhesitatingly he affirmed that 'Principle or Law is God.' There is no doubt about it.*"

In this way, Mahatma Gandhi appreciated the perpetuity of morality and supremacy of God and got inspired by it. Jainism emphasizes on non-violence and Lord Mahavira's dedication to *karmas* and full faith in vegetarianism inspired him inwardly. These inspirations have become an inseparable part of his religion.

Mahatma Gandhi accepted the notion of love and service etc. from Christianity, firm faith in one God and fellow feelings from Islam as an integral part of his religion. But all these practices are the part and parcel of the ancient *Sanatan Dharma*. Forbearance and tolerance along with love, service of mankind, sacrifice and duties etc. form the fundamental principle of *Sanatan* Hindu *Dharma*. He stated :

"*Among all the religions known to me, Hindu religion is the most tolerant. I like the absence of fundamentalism in it, because it gives a chance to its followers for maximum self-expression. To hold reverence for all the religions, to accept all that is good, to follow non-violence, to believe in the oneness of mankind, is the core of Hindu religion as well as of other religions. And this is religion itself that adds to the practical wisdom that one can attain by acting according to the recommended social Varna system. All this can lead to truth, and truth is God. Through it one can serve another. Therefore, I say that my religion is to serve God by serving mankind.*"

Thus, we arrive at the conclusion that Mahatma Gandhi's religion consists of all those fundamental principles, which emerge from Hinduism and assist mankind in its practical welfare. It is inclusive of all the qualities of other prevalent religious communities also. According to *Varnasharama Dharma*, one can follow one's dharma by doing one's duty, as *Shrimad Bhagvad-Gita* also propounds.

God, Truth and Non-violence are just one and the same. The presence of God is truth. Morality is closely associated with God, Truth and Non-violence. In other words, morality is their complementary religion. Besides, Mahatma Gandhi rejected negative aspects like caste, creed, fundamentalism, intolerance, untouchability, and sense of superiority, of any of the religious communities that did not take their followers to the true characteristics of religion.

Religion, according to Mahatma Gandhi, means something, which is adoptable, and that only good is always adoptable. Good is something, which is useful for all and sundry. There is no place for any distinction.

If Mahatma Gandhi was a total believer in the omnipresence of God and both truth and non-violence to be the supplementary principles, he was a superb man of action also.

He had an unflinching faith in karma-the action and to do karma with heart and soul was his religion. He struggled for the freedom of India, for the eradication of distinctions, for the universal brotherhood, for the service of mankind alone and it looks to be his religion. It proves that religion, for him, was not merely a principle, but in inspiring behaviour for the well being of everyone. Besides, truth is a medium to pray to God. Truth is always good and good is that which is attained by the proper means. Therefore, he was justified when he said, "*Non-violence is a true religion.*"

References :

1. On 20-12-1928 he mentioned in Young India, "*God demands nothing less than self-surrender as the price for the only real freedom that is worth having. And when a man thus loses himself, he immediately finds himself in the service of God's creation.*"

2. In this very context Mahatma Gandhi wrote in Young India on 24 November 1927, "*It is my fixed opinion that Buddhism or rather the teaching of Buddha found its full fruition in India and it could not be otherwise, for Gautama was himself a Hindu of Hindus. He was saturated with the best that was in Hinduism, and he gave life to some of the teachings that were buried in the Vedas and which were overgrown with weeds...Buddha never rejected Hinduism, but broadened its base. He gave it a new life and a new interpretation.*"

3. In fact, "*Gautama Buddha*", according to Gandhi, "*rejected the notion that a being called God was actuated by malice, could repent of his actions, and like the kings of earth*

could possibly be open to temptation and bribes and could possible have favourites. His soul rose in mighty indignation against the belief that a being called God required for his satisfaction the living-blood of animals in order that He might be pleased- animal who were His own creation. He, therefore, reinstated God in the right place and dethroned the usurper who for the time being seemed to occupy that White Throne. He emphasized and redeclared the eternal and unalterable existence of the moral government of this universe. He unhesitatingly said that the law was God Himself."

❑❑❑

CHAPTER–2

MAHATMA GANDHI AND POLITICS

Mahatma Gandhi was a person with deep faith in religion. He tried to find answers to various problems of life and world within the parameters of religion and morality. He held the same fervour for all the religious philosophies and their pronouncement, and he spent all his life reinforcing the moral values.

Despite being a religious person, Mahatma Gandhi chose politics as his field of action, but he never gave up moral values even in politics and remained firm and true to the religious discreet. He took religion as a constructive force in politics, and not as a hindrance. Why, because, according to him religion is not merely a philosophy. It is rather a way of life. Religion teaches us how to fulfill the demands of life in true and simple way in our daily practices.

Mahatma Gandhi himself practiced to prove it to us. He was the best representative of all Indian, Indianness, Indian religion and its culture and civilization in his time. He knew very well as to how duty can be followed under all circumstances religiously. In the religion of mankind everything, right from the worship of God to doing everyday chores, is included. And this is the truth of life. The belief of Mahatma that, "*We cannot separate politics from religion*" is justifiable.

NON-BELIEVER

As Mahatma Gandhi stated, "*Without religion a man is like a ship without rudder. Therefore, all my activities, including political, are guided by religion.*"

Mahatma Gandhi's words and the life of any individual around us prove that each one of us is born in a particular religious community, though people are critical of it as well. Once we accept that there is a definite place for religion in life, it will be easier to find its utility and contribution in life and if it is useful, it must have some significance in politics also. That is why, Mahatma Gandhi used to co-relate politics with religion. Whatever doubts are raised about their co-relation, the actions of Gandhi dispelled them automatically. One such example he laid down keeping in mind not only individual life but social life also. There was no public meeting in which Gandhi's address began without a prayer first. He had made it sufficiently clear that only prayer could bring peace and trust in life. In the political field that is the only foundation of all the duties.

ARGUMENT THAT RELIGION AND POLITICS ARE SUPPLEMENTARY

Religion for Mahatma Gandhi consists of impartiality, liberality and values and is dominated by morality. Non-violence and truth are instrumental. In the organization of *Satyagraha*, which inspires man to follow, the path of duty and even the political goal is attained by the same moral, duteous sense of religion. Therefore, Mahatma Gandhi used to say that separation of politics from religion was not advisable. To separate politics from religion, according to him, was an evil practice that should be given up. It, said Gandhi, would be against the directive of the soul. Recommending the co-existence of politics and religion, he argued:

- Religion has been a creative force of human history that has given the moral force to humanity. In this case, the politics will have moral values, when it is related with religion;
- It is not possible to draw a line betwixt man's political-social and religious actions. Therefore, religion, morality and politics cannot be separated. If an attempt is made to separate them, the whole society and human nature would be frequented like the separate parts of human body; and
- Only moral values can shape the character of a man or a nation. As Mahatma Gandhi states, " *Many people say that the ability and efficiency of a person should be meant for guiding his own life through thick and thin, even though he fails to maintain the first rate character on such occasion. But, if the moral excellence is not maintained during the personal achievement, it will be difficult for a person to be true. [In such circumstances] He will not be treated as an honest doer. His potentiality without character can be extremely damaging for the society. Thus, politics without religion will be harmful. Without religion the politicians would be propaGandhists and selfish who will drive their country towards a doom.*"

He further writes, "*In the absence of character, morality and principles based on values, self-governed politicians lose their self assertion and their politics gets corrupted and harmful. In the end they will kill their conscience.*"

Precisely, Mahatma Gandhi approved of the politics characterized with morality. In other words, we can say that he wished to spiritualize politics. His social and political ideas were based on religion and spirituality. It is on this basis that he brought together truth and perseverance *Satyagraha*. It is pertinent to remember that during the freedom struggle of India the religion of Gandhi was to fight for independence. The same *Satyagraha* became his super political policy. During the days of mighty British

Empire, there was no other effective way of opposing it except through the moral force. Thus, to demand justice he had to follow the course of Civil Disobedience.

Secondly, he stood for politics mingled with morality so that good and evil aspects of everything can be fully understood and thus they can fulfill the purpose of Sarvodaya. On these grounds, Mahatma Gandhi was justified when he stated:

"*Religion has been a source of justification in the political activities. So far as I do not treat myself like any other individual, I can lead a religious life and its sense of equality will not germinate in me if I would not have participated in politics. The whole field of human activities is the undivided; in holistic society socio-political and purely religious values cannot be separated. I know no religion except that of the service of mankind. My faith in truth has attracted me to politics, and without hesitation, in full modesty I can state that they, who believe that there is no co-relation betwixt religion and politics, do not know what is religion.*"

Thus, it is clear that Mahatma Gandhi wished to combine values and politics, and this could be possible when it was based on religion. He never wished that in a country like India, there should be any state religion, which was very significant. If we analyze honestly we will see that the political actions based on religious values will enhance the importance of the duties of the State as well as the politics itself. In brief, Mahatma Gandhi's insistence on giving up the non-religious politics was very significant.

❑❑❑

CHAPTER–3

GANDHISM AND PURPOSE AND GOAL OF EDUCATION

Learning is a process. It is a penance. It is such a process and penance that leads a man to the path of progress, peace and successful life. That is why Mahatma Gandhi has remarked :

"*Learning is a never ending constant penance. It moulds human body, mind intellect and character to those tendencies which are key to bliss and proficiency.*"

This is just and appropriate because what is the use of his education if an educated person does not prove helpful in the over-all progress. Therefore, Indian philosophy while accepting the significance of education points out: *SA VIDYA YA VIMUKT AYE*, which means education, results in salvation. This deliverance is not only from the worldly bondage. It paves the way for the ultimate redemption. Mahatma Gandhi, for this reason, chose to declare education as the best of all methods, which should help, in overall mental, physical and intellectual development of a man right from his childhood. This development should prepare his life in such a manner that he may be able to lead a comfortable and peaceful life.

Colleges and universities are the centres of higher learning. It is from the portals of these institutions that students move on to the path of development and social reconstruction after completing their studies. In spite of laying of foundation of learning at the primary and secondary schools, the final decision in respect of the life of students is taken at the college and university levels. Now, in order to understand how education should help to achieve all round development, we shall have comprehensive views of Mahatma Gandhi that he expressed in this regard; especially his views about Indian education are of great significance. He points out:

"*An all round and animated personality both physically and mentally is vibrant and fully aware of his environment. He is desirous of improving it and is capable of taking a decision in this regard... meaning thereby that a man possesses some qualities since his childhood and he adapts himself accordingly with the advancement of his age. The motive of learning is to develop the qualities [of a man] fully so that he may be able to achieve the goals of his life.*"

Only that education shall be considered just which plays decisive role in the achievement of these aims. Mahatma Gandhi has generally suggested basic principles in order to test the correctness of education:

- It should impart practical knowledge;
- It should be capable of determining future goals;
- It should be fully competent to solve the problems;
- It should be proficient enough to make a man self-dependent and self-confident; and
- It should lead a man to spiritualism.

PRACTICAL KNOWLEDGE

Mahatma Gandhi was of the opinion that practical knowledge in life can bring about an all round progress of a student. Therefore, the first and foremost goal of education is to make a student practical in his life. An ideal howsoever lofty has to match to practical learning. Therefore, education must act in order to develop the natural human attributes. In his own words, "*Everyone possesses certain natural virtues from his childhood which are acquired with birth. If these virtues are properly developed their possessor shall certainly grow into a practical person. Such a person will carve out his own path and shall not become a parasite of the society.*" Hence education can prove itself to be meaningful if it tries to shape a student into practical and natural notions.

DETERMINATION OF FUTURE GOAL

The purpose of education should be so clear that it should help the student determine his future goal. An education with an uncertain purpose will render a person's life obscure and puzzling. Therefore, Mahatma Gandhi hails the acquiescence of external mobility along with polishing of one's internal virtues. A student is bound to tread along the path of his life comfortably when he is able to bring about poise in the inner and outer qualities and thus is able to do something for the welfare of the society.

FINDING SOLUTION OF PROBLEMS

Man is a social animal. He cannot be segregated from the society. The development of the society depends upon the progress of man. Thus the goal of education would be that the man, grappling with the social problems, should work for the promotion of society and should develop it into an ideal society, and also, as a part of it should work for the development and awakening of people. That is why Mahatma Gandhi while determining the purpose of education points out that it should aim at perfect fostering of student's intellect so that he may be able to comprehend it thoroughly and then root out the problems.

SELF-CONFIDENCE AND SELF-DEPENDENCE

A student can never be self-dependent if education fails to promote self-confidence in him. This lack of self-dependence shall never let him grow a sense of self-respect thereby denying him any position in life, society and the nation. He can never be expected to set-up a healthy and ideal society. Thus, the goal of education is to make a man self-dependent by developing in him self-confidence.

SPIRITUALISM

Man's path of life cannot become smooth and worth treading by just carving a way of life, determination of future goals, identification of personal and social problems and deliverance therefrom or by becoming self-dependent by developing self-confidence. He must grow physically and mentally to such an extent that he attains perfect health and mobility of character. All this needs spiritualism. Mahatma Gandhi considers spiritualism as an essential ingredient of education and points out that whatever we study and learn in school may help us tread the worldly path successfully but it cannot be considered as complete education. It shall be considered perfect only when it has spiritual aspect too.

Seasoning the qualities of morality, love, justice, chastity, abstinence and self-realization can attain the aspect of spiritualism. Non-violence is the very base of these virtues and is the ultimate truth according to Mahatma Gandhi and truth in his opinion is God.

Thus a student may learn theories through books and may work in laboratories but his education shall be considered complete and perfect only when in order to achieve physical and mental purity, spiritualism is also added to it.

Besides all these goals, Mahatma Gandhi considers equality betwixt man and woman as an essential aim of education. In other words, the real goal of education can never be achieved in the absence of such equality. In addition to this, he recommended mother tongue as the medium of instruction because a student can learn properly through his mother tongue. In case a student is forced to learn through a language other than his mother tongue then in his own words, "*It would result into retardation of his mental growth and burdening him with unnecessary load of books*."

The very essence is that the right trend of education is that which helps the learner to grow physically, mentally and spiritually in perfect manner and thus it can help in all-round development of an individual as well as the society. We have to evaluate the kind of education being imparted in our schools, colleges and universities in context of Mahatma Gandhi's views. We have a number of defects in our traditional type of education and we must investigate them thoroughly and root them out and must identify the system with our objective. Only then we shall be able to achieve our ultimate goals.

Besides, we must understand our system of primary education, and mould it according to our cultural values. Ultimately, education should be perfect and shaped to achieve the aim of an all-round growth of a person. This is the implication of Gandhian system of education.

□□□

CHAPTER–4

GANDHI : NON-VIOLENCE AND DEMOCRACY

Different philosophers, right from Socrates to Karl Marx, have tried to propound foolproof methods of governing people, which should work for the welfare of the commonman, and there is no denying the fact that finding of democratic system of governance can be regarded as the best among all. Since human freedom, equality and justice and welfare of all are the fundamental tenets of democracy, it has come to stay as the best way of governing the people politically.

It is said democracy, as a system of government that started from the small states of Greece about two thousand years ago, has flowed down to us.[1] However, some countries have tried to narrow its meaning to exploit other people, which in fact is absolutely against the very spirit of democratic set up. Keeping such things in view, Mahatma Gandhi-the Father of our nation, made up his mind regarding the concept of democracy, especially for India.[2]

He conceived a democratic set up for India, which would be free from violence so that democracy in this country should be solidly, and purely based on moral and ethical values. Consequently, no one should be able to exploit his fellow men; neither would there be any clash between religion and politics nor would the individual freedom be under any threat. Moreover, with the adoption of non-violent means Indians should be able to see mankind achieve pinnacles of glory and growth and thus accomplish the ultimate goal of universal peace and brotherhood.

For the accomplishment of a democratic set up free from violence, Mahatma Gandhi put forward his considered views. He refused to accept the democracy adopted by the west as absolute, fixed and meaningful because according to him, the democracy as it comes to be established there had its basis on violence and exploitation of fellow beings. Thus, in the issue of *Harijan Sewak* dated 12 November 1938 he emphasized:

"*Democracy and violence can never go together. The countries that are democracies just for the name, either should clearly support dictatorship or they should be bold enough to adopt the path of non-violence if they wish to be called true democracies. I am of the opinion that democracies in the Western countries are just for the name. They may have some aspects of true democracies but they cannot be called so unless they embark on the tenets of non-violence. Such a situation will relieve them of much trouble and nuisance. For the proper growth of democracy, there can be no compromise with violence and falsehood.*"

While analyzing human nature and the growth of the world, Mahatma Gandhi opines, "*Man by nature is fond of power and this fondness of man ends with his death. Therefore, it is very difficult to put under control the young man honking after power. We do not find any institution [fully] based on non-violence. Democracy cannot be considered perfect until it is found to be based on the foundation of non-violence. It is, therefore, necessary to practice non-violence in our day-to-day actions and by doing so we are bound to succeed in our mission.*"

Mahatma Gandhi has very frankly and openly expressed his opinion regarding fundamentals of democracy such as:

DEMOCRACY AND MAJORITY OPINION

Mahatma Gandhi wants the establishment of democracy through moral development of men and with the help of the weapon of non-violence. He is of very strong opinion that although the principle of majority has nothing to do with what is based on conscience yet in the modern practical democracy, this principle of majority is used in a very narrow sense. We may bow to majority opinion put surrounding to it on every count would mean its slavery. Democracy does not render human beings to act as mere sheep. It protects the freedom of judgement and the action of people.

DEMOCRACY AND FREEDOM

Mahatma Gandhi considered freedom like a birth. Till we are fully free, we are slaves. But he felt that true freedom could only be achieved through non-violent means. It means that the use of untrue and violent means would naturally crush the opponents and their views. Individual freedom that according to him is the most important thing in human life,[3] in such a situation, cannot be protected. It can maintain itself during a purely non-violent democratic set up.

Individual freedom and non-violence are to democracy just as the spinal cord is to human body. It is, therefore, imperative for the government to project and defend individual freedom. However, one should make use of one's power in such a manner that it does not interfere with the freedom of one's neighbours. In the words of Mahatma Gandhi, "Every individual is a part of his nation or his society and is, therefore, supposed not to make use of his powers for his individual self but for the society on which he is dependent."

DEMOCRACY AND EQUALITY

In 1935 Mahatma Gandhi wrote in the Harijan that inequality has no place in democracy. Inequality is an evil, but I do not believe in relieving a man of it by fear or force. Inequality should be removed only at the national level. Those nations who talk ill of democracy have no right to consider other nations as inferior. The consideration of high and low gives birth to violence. A democracy based on non-violence lays emphasis on equality among individuals and nations.

DEMOCRACY AND RIGHT TO VOTE

Right to vote plays a major role in a democracy. Mahatma Gandhi favours the right to vote to be established through non-violent method. In his words, "*The government which have its base on non-violence cannot claim to be a democratic government. On the contrary it would be far more important than the right to vote if the government puts the majority will into practice and every action is aimed at the welfare of the common masses.*"

DEMOCRACY AND LAW

Mahatma Gandhi believes strongly in the change of heart of the guilty instead of punishing him in a violent manner. Democratic set up as a punishing authority and democracy do not go together. His opinion about such a democracy indicates that a power born out of non-violence is mightier than the power of states based on the strength of their weapons put together. In fact, if the democratic governments try to practice non-violence to the maximum the least they shall have to fall back upon the legal intricacy because "*there can be no enemy of democracy based on non-violence.*"

DEMOCRACY AND DECENTRALIZATION

Mahatma Gandhi considered centralization of power as a serious threat to democracy. The tendency of centralization symbolizes violent power, and violence has no place in democracy. Supporters of democracy based on violence can never respect the voice of the commonman. There should be decentralization in the field of economic activities because the policy of economic centralization gives birth to selfishness, which further propels exploitation brought about by imperialism.

A country can never be called a true democracy if it believes in militarization, imperialism, and colonialism or has faith in resources, which cause violence or otherwise supports, or sympathizes with the nations following such principles. Besides, the government of a country cannot be considered to be a true democratic government which believes in centralization of power and the government, too, cannot be considered purely democratic which otherwise being cowardly claim to be non-violent; try to avoid self purification and moral promotion and do not believe in true and non-violent set up. Mahatma Gandhi possessed lofty ideas in this regard. His strong and fundamental perception provides strength to a perfect form of government i.e. democracy. Besides, this perception shows mankind a right and peaceful path to live.

Reference:

1. In fact, the history of democracy in India dates back to ancient times. Although it is generally assumed that democratic system was first started in city-states of Greece but if we study the history of India, we find that it did not first start there. The villages in India which are the lowest units, enjoyed autonomy in ancient India; their chiefs were elected. During the times of Gautama Buddha, there were many self-governing communities and federations whose leaders were elected. They were republics. Buddha's father Shuddhodana was a

member of Shakya republican system of government and in the same capacity was proclaimed a king also.

2. In this context Mahatma Gandhi clarified in 1920, "*The spirit of democracy is not a mechanical thing to be adjusted by abolition of forms. It requires change of the heart.... [It] requires the inculcation of the spirit of brotherhood.*" Further he said, " *Democracy must in essence... mean the art and science of mobilizing the entire physical, economic and spiritual resources of all the various sections of the people in the service of the common good of all.*"

3. About Individual freedom Mahatma Gandhi said, "*If this [individual liberty] goes, then surely all is lost, for, if the individual ceases to count, what is left for society? Individual freedom alone can make a man voluntarily surrender himself completely to the service of society. If it is wrested from him, he becomes an automation and society is ruined. No society can possibly be built on a denial of individual freedom. It is contrary to the very nature of man. Just as a man will not grow horns or tail, so he will not exist as man if he has no mind of his own. In reality, even those who do not believe in the liberty of the individual believe in his or her own. Modern editions of Chenghiz Khan retain their own.*"

□□□

CHAPTER–5

RELIGION IN POLITICS : CONSTRUCTIVE OR DESTRUCTIVE

Religion is not merely a philosophical study but it is a way of life; it is a necessity to identify one with the whole mankind. To Mahatma Gandhi it is dearer than his country.[1] It is not a formal thing, or customary.[2] Religion teaches us how to live our daily life in a practical manner. Mahatma Gandhi exhaustively dealt with this subject in its entire ramification, in the context of our country. In finding an answer to the question whether the role of religion in politics is constructive, I would quote Mahatma Gandhi who, in his times, represented whole of India, its religion, culture and civilization in the best possible manner. That's why; in my opinion there could not be a better exponent of this subject than the Mahatma.

"*A man without religion is like a ship without a rudder*," these are Mahatma Gandhi's words. He confessed, "*My politics and all other activities of mine are derived from my religion*." However, certain people may decry religion, it must be remembered that every one is born with a religion. Once we concede that religion is a necessity in every one's life, it is then easy to concede that religion in politics has meaningful purpose. In fact it is very necessary. Thus, the religion in politics is constructive and not destructive was proved beyond any shadow of doubt by his activities by Gandhi. In this regard he several times set noble examples in his personal life as well as in public life, which we may easily find in the pages of contemporary history of India i.e. the history of national liberation movement of India of Gandhian era.

Mahatma Gandhi made it clear, "*Politics bereft of religion is absolutely dirt, ever to be shunned. Politics divorced from religion has absolutely no meaning. We draw no hard and fast line of demarcation between political, social, religious and other questions. Human life being an undivided whole no line could ever be drawn between its different components, nor between ethics and politics.*"

It was after well justifying the place of religion in politics that Mahatma Gandhi began to explain that his life was dedicated to service of India through religion and non-violence that he believed to be at the root of Hinduism. In this very context, he very rightly interpreted Hinduism in these words, "*Hinduism is not an exclusive religion. In it there is room for the worship of all the prophets in the world, for Hinduism had absorbed the best of all faiths of the world and in that sense Hinduism was not an exclusive religion.*"

It is religion that gives a spiritual force to man in his personal life or in society or in movement. Let us remember today that it was this spiritual force that gave a strong impetus to our freedom movement. The deafening cries of the mantra *VANDE MATARAM* rent the air in those days, when the people gathered round our leaders, and marched forward. It was that collective prayer, the call of our *BHARAT MATA*, which was fully responsible for taking us on the road to victory ultimately. Did not the people non-violently fight for their freedom? It was the religion of non-violence that Mahatma Gandhi preached to Indians and practiced himself.

Mahatma Gandhi studied all the scriptures of the world deeply and absorbed the essence of all of them. Also he thoroughly studied the condition of the people, understood their basic problems in the background of their faith and culture and came to the conclusion that religion can definitely be of great help to root out the problems of masses. He found truth and ahimsa the basis of all the faiths. That is why he declared, "*Truth is my religion and ahimsa is the only way of its realization. Dharma is one and only one. Ahimsa means Moksha and Moksha is the realization of truth. Belief in one God is the touch stone of all faiths...*"

The influence of religion on the minds of our other great leaders is well known. We may quote patriots like Bal Gangadhar Tilak, Aurobindo, Rajagopalachari, Subramanyam Bharti and others who being public leaders were fully influenced by religion.

Not only Hinduism but other major faiths of the world too call upon to mingle connection of politics with religion. In this connection it is relevant to draw attention to the views expresses by American philosopher George Santayana who says that inter-play of religion and politics is well illustrated in the fortunes of the Hebraic faith. He proceeds to say to the extent, "*Religion and politics thus come into the world together like twins; and it is not unlikely that religion may have been the first born.*"

We all know that Jesus Christ brought the Kingdom of Heaven on earth, and Christianity became the official faith in many countries of the world. Before Christ, Buddhism as a reformist- religion, based on compassion-a value supplementary to ahimsa, influenced the monarchs of India like Ashoka-the Great, in whose time it spread to other far-eastern countries as well. The same is to be said that Jainism, which fully revolves around *ahimsa* played constructive role in Indian politics in our own times under the leadership of Mahatma Gandhi, is now a matter of recorded history.

Since one meaning of the word *dharma*, that is known, as religion is itself to bind, it is our duty to employ it for constructive purpose. In the name of religion, politics should not divide us, but religion should bind us together, for playing our constructive role in politics. It is only that religion can justify its place in politics and politics can be constructed with the help of religion for the benefit of the people.

The faith of joining millions of Indians is strongly rooted in God and religion. It is religion that unites the whole of our India as one spiritual and cultural entity. Even though attempts may be made by some persons to mislead the people in regard to the role of religion in national life. Some religious fanatics may try to bring about destructive results in the political life of the nation, but we have every confidence that the vast majority of our people will not allow themselves to be deceived or deluded by such vicious propagandas and they will use religion as an instrument for forging national unity and for doing constructive work. We say this because even our saints- to whatever part they belong and whatever language they speak-have been also social reformers. Take the case of Swami Vivekananda for instance. He was a social reformer par excellence, and he rightly and repeatedly said to proceed on the path of dharma and taught to work with religious fervour for upliftment of people. He called upon Indians to ensure to work in this direction and to show this correct path to the rest of world too.

No nation can function well unless it has character. The character of a nation is ultimately the character of individuals that reflect it. Many friends tell us that measure a man's efficiency and don't bother about his private life. I feel that character must have priority over efficiency. Efficiency without character is always socially dangerous. So politics without character is always socially dangerous; ultimately without religion politics is more dangerous to society. In short, politics without religion will breed unscrupulous, intriguing and characterless leaders that will lead to disaster of the nation. That is why Mahatma Gandhi's advocacy for togetherness of religion and politics is considerable.

Reference:

1. In this context Mahatma Gandhi has written in Young India on 23-02-1922, "*There is undoubtedly a sense in which the statement is true when I say that I hold my religion dearer than my country and that, therefore, I am Hindu first and nationalist after. I do not become on that score less a nationalist than the best of them. I simply thereby imply that the interests of my country are identical with those of my religion. Similarly, when I say that I prize my own salvation above everything else, above the salvation of India, it does not mean that my personal salvation requires a sacrifice of India's political or any other salvation. But it implies necessarily that the two go together.*"

2. In the words of Gandhi himself, "*By religion, I do not mean formal religion, or customary religion, but that religion which underlies all religions, which brings us face to face with our Maker.*" This religion of Mahatma Gandhi has no geographical limits. It is not a prison-house; it, of course, has room for the least among God's creation. His religion binds one indissolubly to the truth within and which ever purifies. On May 12, 1920, he wrote in Young India, "*Let me explain what I mean by religion. It is not the Hindu religion which I certainly prize above all other religions, but the religion which transcends Hinduism, which changes one's very nature, which binds one indissolubly to the truth within and which ever purifies. It is the permanent element in human nature that counts no cost too great in order to find full expression and which leaves the soul utterly restless until it has found itself, known its Maker and appreciated the true correspondence between the maker and itself.*"

□□□

CHAPTER–6

GANDHI : EDUCATION AND PEACE

There is some purpose behind the creation. If we accept the view that there is no purpose behind human creation, our life will become simply meaningless. We must accept the idea of purposefulness whether we are atheists or theists. Be it Lord Buddha or Lord Mahavira, Prophet Mohammed or Lord Jesus Christ, everyone was of the singular opinion that there was a purpose in the creation of mankind on this planet. There may be differences of opinion so far as the mode of purpose is concerned but each one of them agreed on the issue of the purpose of human creation.

Now, the main issue under consideration is to understand this purpose. All the great philosophers unanimously agree that the main purpose of life is to establish peace. Thus the fundamental issue of human life is to bring about peace and to live in peace. That is why the ultimate aim of life is to achieve salvation or redemption so that after leading a peaceful life the soul should also rest in peace.

It is not possible to make human life peaceful while passing through trials and tribulations of individuals and social problems, pains and pleasure being essentially associated with them. While undergoing all these experiences we have to pave our path with peace. Lord Buddha, Lord Mahavira, Prophet Mohammed, Lord Jesus Christ, Confucius, Zoroaster and Nanak, all of them after leading their human lives and undergoing all such experiences, were able to give us a message of peace.

Progress and development are inseparably attached to peace. By the terms progress and development I mean the progress and all-around development of this world. Our internal struggles, differences of opinion and jealousies become meaningless when we realize that the ultimate aim of human life is to achieve peace. Thus, it clearly means that the existence of internal struggles, differences of opinion and jealousies amongst us amply indicate that we have failed to understand the true aim or purpose of life, or that we are unable to understand this aim. Thus our immediate need is first to comprehend the real and ultimate motives of life. Therefore, we need to be properly educated in the comprehension of our aims and motives. In fact we shall become clear about our view of life if we are imparted the right kind of education. Great humanist and the Father of the Indian Nation, Mahatma Gandhi defines education in a proper manner. He considers it to be the bedrock of an all-around development of man, which will ultimately decide the final aim of human life with all the desired prosperity and joys.

According to Gandhi, education is an unending exercise till death. Only it can act as a means to the end of a successful life. It can help to mould and shape human body, mind and character in such a manner that they may act as means to achieve joys and efficiency. Gandhi who happened to be great humanist thought of man as a great self-dependent creature. That is why he did not restrict the definition of education into narrow limits. He did not restrict it to the boundaries of a nation and rather considered it to be global in its character. He considered it to be such a source that could smoothen human life right from birth till death and finally helped to achieve salvation so that the soul could embrace an everlasting peace.

We shall be able to comprehend Gandhi's views of education better if we go through the following words of Kishorelal Mashruwala:

"... *That it works for the all-around growth of man right*

from the beginning till the end. Its ultimate aim is to turn human knowledge into his ability... It is not meant for his life and not only for earning his livelihood..."

Thus education is clearly a process, which helps an all-around growth of man. This growth ultimately directs him to the achievement of the only aim - peace.

Although Gandhi laid emphasis on the imparting of education according to ancient Indian culture yet it is of a great significance in the modern times. His standards of education had been fixed with Indian perspective in his mind but they instruct the world community as a whole as well and their application is of great significance even today as it had done in .the past and they are bound to be useful for the future generations as well.

In the context of education he had affirmed that it should be useful enough to make man fully self-dependent and should fix his future aim; besides it should make him competent enough to find solution to his day-to-day problems. It should direct his life in such a manner that after attaining mental and physical qualities he should become rightful claimant of salvation. The education with all these qualities can be considered the true education.

Our primary schools, high schools, colleges and universities impart education. After obtaining education from the portals of these institutions, the people enter their future life. Thus this is our bounden duty to impart education as visualized by Gandhi. Only then can we achieve the true aim of education and tread the path leading to the achievement of ultimate peace.

Educationists will accede to this logic that modern education system is insensitive to its basic aims. Here I want to emphasize that this system is indifferent to human problems. Man is bound to remain unhappy till he is surrounded by these problems. How can peace be established in such a situation? This is the biggest drawback of our educational system that it is unable to solve the fundamental human problems. Although this is true that our educational system is getting modernized with the introduction of computer and other achievements in the technological field yet it has not been able to achieve its aim.

In order to achieve the aims of education we must ponder over the views expressed by Gandhi. In this context I would like to mention here in brief three points with a view to mould our educational system according to them. Our schools, colleges and universities must impart education on these lines.

Firstly, education must be according to the conduct of human beings. Gandhi was of the view that man has some natural and inherent qualities since childhood. If these qualities are developed with the help of education, man can achieve self-dependence. At first children must be made to learn alphabet. Besides they must be made aware of their duties towards their country and society. However, later on their inherent qualities must be made to grow and develop and then only they will certainly be able to fulfill their aim if the educational system is evolved accordingly.

Secondly, I would like to mention about technical[1] or vocational education. Imparting of literary knowledge is not the be-all and end-all of education. It involves moral, mental and physical growth of man. Thus technical education is of permanent importance besides literary knowledge. We must add this education to the syllabi at college stage. Otherwise this method of education is not going to help any more. Even if we try to stick to it, we shall not be doing justice to our students. Thus one such subject has to be added to the syllabi so that a student is able to get a job immediately after he becomes a graduate.

As the Vice-Chancellor, I myself had recommended the introduction of seven such subjects but they were introduced at the post graduation level. I am happy that the Chancellor has recently issued instructions for the introduction of these subjects proposed by me. Among these subjects are Journalism,

Biotechnology, Glass technology, Seed production and M.B.A. etc. These are the forms of technical education.

Thirdly, about spiritualism. Gandhi, in fact, was a religious person and by the introduction of spiritual education he meant to achieve proximity to the Almighty. But even otherwise as well, spiritual education is of great importance because moral upliftment of man is essential. Without moral upliftment man ceases to be a real man. Thus even an atheist needs to be trained in spiritual education, though it may be in term of moral education.

There is an immortal proverb in the context of education where it has been affirmed that only education can help to achieve salvation. This salvation is not only in the context of leading a successful life in the mortal world but it ensures success even after death. Education must play an important role in leading man to salvation and providing undisturbed peace to the human soul. Only then shall education be complete and only then shall it become a means for the achievement of ultimate peace.

Gandhi held this view. He strongly believed that man is neither a mental state, nor a physical state, nor is he simply a soul. All these states added together help to bring about the unit, which is known as man. Education is a means to make a human being of that man and the ultimate aim is the achievement of peacefulness.

Reference:

1. For it, Mahatma Gandhi has used the term 'Basic' or '*Buniyadi*'. In this connection he wrote in both the Young India and Harijan several times. In the Young India of[1] September 1921, he wrote, "*The introduction of manual training will serve a double purpose in a poor country like ours. It will pay for the education of our children and teach them an occupation on which they can fall back*

in after-life, if they choose, for earning a living. Such a system must make our children self-reliant. Nothing will demoralize the nation so much as that we should learn to despise labour." In this very context he also emphasized upon self-supporting education making industrial training as a compulsory part of it. [See Appendix-A for details.]. In Harijan dated 2-11-1947, Mahatma Gandhi suggested following six fundamentals of Basic/*Buniyadi* Education also:

- All education to be true must be self-supporting, that is to say, in the end it will pay its expenses excepting the capital which will remain intact;
- In it the cunning of the hand will be utilized even up to final stage, that is to say, hands of the pupils will be skillfully working at some industry for some period during the day;
- All education must be imparted through the medium of the provincial language;
- In this there is no room for giving sectional religious training. Fundamental universal ethics will have full scope;
- This education, whether it is confined to children or adults, male or female, will find its way to the homes of the pupils; and
- Since millions of students receiving this education will consider themselves as of the whole of India, they must learn an inter-provincial language. This common inter-provincial speech can only be Hindustani written in *Nagri* or *Urdu* script. Therefore, pupils have to master both the scripts.

□□□

CHAPTER–7

THE SIGNIFICANCE OF GANDHISM IN THE ESTABLISHMENT OF PEACE

I wished to present my views on some aspect of Indology. But my friend Prof. Göhler desired me to express my opinion on some subject concerning Gandhian thought. Since world peace is my favourite subject of study, I ventured into expressing my views on the significance of Gandhism in the establishment of peace. I do not claim to be an expert of Gandhian thought. I am yet trying to fathom his philosophy. During the past seventeen years I have been making efforts to delve into Gandhism. This effort of mine is a humble expression of whatever little I have been able to assimilate.

I hope you would agree with me that an effort to establish peace has been the only motive of man. During every age and at every place people have been making endeavours for the achievement of this aim. It is immaterial how far these efforts have borne fruits.. But after all why have all these efforts been made? The simple answer is for the comfortable existence and prosperity of mankind. This is a fact that it is only during peace that mankind can prosper and flower. That is why great men have made efforts for the establishment of global peace. Gandhi also did so. He worked tirelessly for the achievement of world peace! So much so, that he has left some principles behind him, the following of which can assure the achievement of peace in the struggle-torn world of today. It would be proper to consider the Gandhian philosophy that can certainly help to establish a regime of peace.

Gandhi based his deeds or action and thoughts on non-violence. Considering it a religion[1] and also the law of the human race,[2] he is of the strong opinion that non-violence is the only means to establish peace.[3] He is also of the view that non-violence is eternal. It is such a necessity of the society that must go on growing. It is a permanent part of human temperament. This is why we could advance and progress. Otherwise, man would always go through constant tortures resulting, into the absolute removal of existence of mankind from the earth.

In order to establish his point Gandhi gave example of the primitive men when they used to kill and eat one another. Later on they started preying upon the animals for their flesh. Now man started digging the ground and growing food from the land. Instead of leading a gypsy life, he settled down at a place and villages and towns came into existence. It is a sign of successive rise of non-violence. The spirit of violence started becoming lesser. Had it not been so, the human race would by now have become extinct.

Thus non-violence is a great necessity of human life and Gandhism calls for the growth and development of non-violence and the allied instincts. This would certainly pave the way for peace, which is ultimate goal of human life. Supporting his stand he had opined that all the great prophets and religious leaders have supported non-violence. None has preached violence. How could they support it? There is no need to preach violence. Animal instincts present in man make him violent. But as a soul he is non-violent. When the soul has an upper hand, man ceases to be violent. Either he will learn non-violence or he shall cease to exist at all. That is why great men and prophets preached unity, justice, brotherhood, truth and self-control. All these help to develop non-violence and peace. Therefore, for the establishment of peace, comfort and prosperity, it would be our responsibility to establish nonviolence on the individual and social levels. At first the growth of individual violent thoughts will have to be curbed. Later, we shall have to bring the family, the society, the nation and finally the group of nations on to the same line. If we do not act accordingly and are unable to control violence, what would be our fate? History can teach us great lessons. We have fought two destructive wars in this century and their results are before us.

The First World War lasted a little more than four years from 1st August 1914 to 11th November 1918. About ten million young men were killed and another 22.5 million were injured in that war. At that time the world population stood at 175 million. What was the result of this war? 1225 million people were thrown into a miserable condition. They became a victim of the torture inflicted by colonization. There was no question of the development of any area of the world. Besides, it took more than a decade for the warring countries to come back to the path of progress. This was a very simple instance of the result of war among nations.

The Second World War lasted for 6 years i.e. 1939 to 1945. But could it achieve anything in the name of peace and could such a violent war solve any problem? The warring nations were badly tired in the end. Their progress came to a stand still. Tired of the violence, those nations started looking for peace. This was quite natural because what they derived from war is worth knowing particularly as it is of much significance for the present generation.

This war resulted into the killing of 50 million people. About 35 million people were injured and colossal amount equivalent to 1117 million U.S. Dollars were spent on the warfare. The developmental work in the whole of the world came to a grinding halt. Besides it took the nations another 15 years to move on to the path of progress: What did this war result into is worth considering? Had only a quarter of this amount being spent on peaceful measures and the solution of different' disputes arising between different parties, it would certainly have shown spectacular results.

Take the example of the USSR. Twenty million of its people were killed and 1700 towns and 70,000 villages were completely destroyed. It suffered a loss of the destruction of 30,000 industrial units, 4 thousand railway stations and sixty thousand kilometer of railway lines. So much so, 70 millions of heads of cattle also perished in this war. The war had a dampening effect on the developmental activities of the nation for the next 20 years and the country suffered a loss of 26,000 million roubles.

In case of Germany, the human loss stood at 12.5 million. On the front of arms and ammunition this war claimed its one hundred thousand aeroplanes, 25 thousand tanks and 2 hundred thousand guns.

Britain lost its 3.3 hundred thousand soldiers, 60 thousand civilians and 1.9 hundred thousand others. It lost thirty thousand of its merchant navy personnel. Nine million residential houses besides industrial units worth 51, 500 million pound sterling were, completely destroyed.

Almost all the nations involved in this war suffered more or less the same magnitude of losses. The warring nations brought the whole world to the brink of an absolute devastation. Violence shocked everybody. They aspired for peace, which resulted into unending moves! For useful dialogues, agreements and treaties.

All of us know that after abdication of violence, the Leagues of Nations was found as a step towards the search for world peace after World War First. Similarly, U.N.O. came into existence after the World War Second. Despite all political activity being done at the platform of the U.N.O. and in spite of all the apprehensions being expressed regarding the role of U.N.O., it has been playing its role in the direction of maintaining world peace very meaningfully.

Gandhism emphasizes the adoption of non-violent means. Differences of opinion among people are quite natural but these differences have to be resolved through dialogues, agreements and treaties. Thus growth of non-violence and its operatives in the human nature are of paramount importance for the existence and prosperity of mankind. They had been essential and they are equally essential even today. The historians are well aware of the war fought between the Athenians and Spartans some two thousand five hundred years ago. This war lasted for ten years [431 B.C. - 421 B.C.]. The Commanders of the two states Brasidus and Klion were killed. The two states at last had to reach a mutually agreed understanding and students of history are very much aware of this treaty as the Treaty of Nisious.

The first war of Punic lasted for 23 years from 264 B. C. to 241 B. C. Violence left them helpless, pitiable and tired. They were left with no option but to forsake violence and arrive at a peaceful solution, which was affected by the treaty in 241 B.C.

Again in 218 B.C., Second War of Punic broke out. This time it lasted for 17 years but it also met the same fate as that of the first war of Punic. Rome and Carthage, the belligerent parties entered into a peace treaty in 202 B.C., which is known as the "*Treaty of Jama*". But the warring parties did not adhere to the conditions laid down in this treaty and Carthage became a victim of violence. However, the Republic of Rome failed to extract any permanent advantage of its victory over Carthage. How could violence, an inhuman characteristic become a source of lasting and permanent happiness? I need not repeat what happened later. Every historian is well aware of it.

If we look at Europe of the first decade of the 19th Century we shall find many countries, the important among them being England, France and Russia, involved in the frenzy of war. For two years from 1805-07, they were fully involved in warfare, which left them badly tired. Now they wanted to establish peace. They depended upon the non-violent means of meetings and dialogues, which culminated into welcome results. Napoleon and Alexander arrived at an understanding and the "*Treaty of Tilsit*" was its result.

Do you need more instances? If so, many more of them can be cited. Look at the hostilities between Russia and France in 1872. Around one hundred renowned army commanders of the day and hundred of thousands of soldiers were killed in these hostilities. Napoleon could achieve only partial and temporary victory over Russia. But what did it all result into? Everybody is aware of it. Whenever, the warring nations leaving violence headed towards non-violent solutions the results were certainly pleasant and joyful. Peace was restored and it added to the happiness and prosperity of mankind. Non-violence is such a wealth. That is why Mahatma

Gandhi and his ideology consider non-violence to be supremc for world peace.

Non-violence is a noble and truthful means to achieve noble, truthful and permanent ends. Gandhiji appealed for the adoption of truthful and non-violent means and it was only through these that a truly peaceful universe could become a reality. Violence may achieve success but it shall certainly be temporary and deceptive. Such a success shall be short-lived, distressing and sorrowful. He opined that means are of greater importance. Means would definitely control the ends. Means and ends can never be separated. Almighty has empowered us to control the means, which are otherwise very limited. The ends shall certainly become virtuous and noble in agreement with the means. These words of Gandhi are potent enough to make it clear that the achievement made through non-violent means are permanent and truthful and for the well being of all and one. Thus Gandhism is an appeal to mankind for the establishment of peace through non-violence. This solicitation is potent and efficacious and timely even today. Hence Gandhism too is an effective and convincing force for the installation of peace all over the world.

INDIVIDUAL & SOCIAL NON-VIOLENCE:

A very significant question can be raised in the context of nonviolence and that too in its role in the installation of peace. Since non-violence is an individual trait, how can it be helpful at social, national and international levels? In this context he had pointed out that non-violence is not only an individual attribute, it is a social feature too; therefore, it should be developed as a social characteristic like other human traits[4] and has to be accepted that the regulation of social interactions is broadly brought about through non-violence.[5] He wanted this principle to be extended to national and international levels.

He wanted non-violence to be developed into a social attribute beginning it from the individual level. This is not a difficult task as society is a composition of individuals what is required is consistent efforts in this direction. The continuances of such efforts are likely to bear fruit in the form of final establishment of peace.

In the 3rd December, 1938 issue of "*The Harijan*", Gandhi penned a lengthy article wherein he dwelt not only on the establishment of a non-violent society but declared it to be of paramount importance for human comfort, peace and prosperity. He declared it to be the ultimate aim of human life. Emphasizing its necessity he said that the installation of such a society was positively conceivable. In this article he remarked that it had become a fashion to point out the installation and furtherance of a society based on the principles of non-violence impractical but he said that he was strongly opposed to such a thesis. In this context he has pointed out that in a family, a father chastises his son for his wrongful act but the son does not even imagine retaliating. The son bears the chastisement, as he knows that it was the result of his father's hurt affection, which compelled him to take that action. He was of the view that the social set-up should also be on the similar lines. Family is a small unit of the society. What is true of a family is true of a society as well because society is a bigger family.

NON-VIOLENCE & COWARDLINESS:

Gandhism while considering non-violence as a supreme value, separates it from cowardliness, it calls upon man never to be cowardly and also not to disassociate himself from non-violence. Both can never go together. It clearly asks a man neither to bow to cowardliness nor to fall a victim to exploitation while adopting non-violence as way of life. India's struggle for freedom under the leadership of Gandhi is a stellar example of a non-violent struggle against tyranny, injustice and exploitation. Gandhi provided leadership to the movement of India's struggle for freedom for about 30 years [1917-47]. During this period he launched a non-violent movement for rooting out slavery besides other injustices from which Indian people were suffering and the favourable and pleasant results of that movement are very much before the people of the world, Gandhi and his followers never showed any cowardliness while fighting against tyranny, injustice or exploitation. The reason was very evident. The adoption of non-violence in their life had raised the morale of freedom fighters to such lofty heights that never portrayed any fear of cowardliness and it had strengthened moral courage to such an extent that the question of buckling to the principle of injustice would not arise. Gandhi felt that non-violence had such a glorious feature that the oppressor would finish himself if he could not remove injustice; the oppressor would either be compelled to rectify his mistake or would find himself lonely in the face of a non-violent struggle.

Thus it can be concluded that the solution of a problem or a controversy is possible to rectify all the ills. It is, therefore, advisable to start a meaningful dialogue in a hostile condition, be it individual, familial, social, national or international, and then enter into an agreement or have a treaty. This is what Gandhi or his philosophy of non-violence teaches us. On the contrary, violence has brought nothing to the world except annihilation. I affirm with conviction and history also supports it, I have placed before you a number of instances from history and am ready to quote many more such instances if desired.

History witnesses 116 years long war [1337-1453] betwixt France and England but what did they achieve from it? What they gained was a loss of manpower and wealth. Similarly, China attacked Korea many times between 598 A. D. to 660 A. D. but could achieve nothing through the use of brutal force.

It is high time we thought over the problem and worked for the establishment of peace through non-violent means as professed by Gandhi. This is the need of the day; there is no alternative to nonviolence. Lord Buddha too preached the adoption of three ideals in our day-to-day behaviour for the establishment of an ideal society. These three ideals are as under:

- We shall never resort to violence;
- We shall never partake violence; and
- We shall never support the person having recourse to violence.

How lofty these ideals are! We shall be doing much for the welfare of the society if we while adopting them in true letter and spirit practice the fourth ideal too. The fourth ideal being, "*We shall at once overcome the violent feeling as and when it emerges in mind and in case it does erupt we shall never let it spread*". By adopting these principles we shall follow the footsteps of Gandhi and shall be making an enormous contribution to the installation of peace, which is truth, and prime need of the hour.

Reference:

1. Considering ahimsa as the religion in grandeur, applicable for all, Mahatma Gandhi said, "*I am not a visionary. I claim to be a practical idealist. The religion of non-violence is not meant merely for the rishis and saints. It means for the common people as well. Non-violence is the law of our species as violence is the law of the brute. The spirit lies dormant in the brute and he knows no law but that of physical might. The dignity of man requires obedience to a higher law-to the strength of the spirit....*"

2. Defining the character of non-violence, Mahatma Gandhi wrote in Harijan on 5th September 1936, "*Non-violence is the law of the human race and is definitely greater than and superior to brute force.*"

3 In this context he said to the extent that non-violence is the only condition of survival of India. And in case "*India makes violence her creed, and I have survived, I would not care to live in India. She will cease to evoke any pride in me.*"

4. Non-violence is a permanent human instinct. It is present in every human being. Since society comprises of human beings, it is imperative that after developing this characteristic in individuals, efforts should be made for its development in the society as a whole.

5. Despite the existence of co-operation and struggle side by side the spirit of cooperation in the society is supreme. In its absence the society shall cease to exist. In the case of a family, husband, the head of the family, works hard throughout the day to earn his livelihood, which helps him, acquire different

things of necessity. The son goes out to fetch the fuel wood. The wife does the domestic chores and the daughter helps her in it. Now the food products brought by the husband, fuel wood collected by the son and with the help of wife and daughter the food is cooked after which all of them sit together and eat it. The whole of this process is based on mutual love and co-operation. The same is true of the society. Each member of it is dependent on the other. The same truth applies to a nation and in fact to the whole of the world. The basic sentiment working in the background of this all is non-violence in the absence of which the family shall get disintegrated. The society and the nation too will disintegrate and the very existence of the universe shall become questionable.

❑❑❑

CHAPTER–8

GANDHISM AND CONFLICT RESOLUTION AT THE CLOSE OF 20th CENTURY

First of all, I express gratitude towards your Institute, which has accorded an opportunity to me to be before you to express my views on '*Gandhism & Conflict Resolution at the close of 20th Century*'.

The topic is really quite in tune with time because we are now standing on the verge of the close of this century, obviously 20th century, in which there have been severe conflicts including two world wars. Approximately 150 million people lost their lives in these and the same number pertains to those who were injured. There were innumerable amongst the injured that could survive but their life was reduced to a position worse than that of death. I have no data relating to the loss of property. I also do not possess any data concerning the quantum of obstacles in developmental activities, which resulted owing to these. I can, however, firmly state that there was destruction. Humanity was fully ignored. No one could gain anything. Everyone was at loss: more or less. Those who portray some gain out of all these things are wrong. Nothing can be permanently achieved out of a war or conflict.

Before initiating a further discourse on '*Gandhism and conflict resolution at the close of 20eth century*' it is essential for us to know what Gandhism ultimately happens or remains to be. Broadly, Gandhism is precise or abridged form of those views which Mahatma Gandhi put before humanity in this world. He practised these views by exercising them in his life. The views undoubtedly become very much significant when one, who expresses them, treads them in life. It is so with Mahatma Gandhi. His views are acclaimed today not only in India but also in the whole world. What are these views? What do they incorporate so as to become significant the world over? The reply is that these views call upon human beings to live and let live-*JIO AUR JINE DO*. These views oppose conflict of every kind and propagate mutual cooperation in every sphere. While opposing conflict and calling upon mutual cooperation, the centre point of his views is non-violence. Existence of every living being, not only of human being, is based on non-violence.

What is non-violence? It is non and violence that is abstinence from violence when we analyze the word. Broadly, it means not depriving some one of life. In elaborated terms, it means not causing violence per thought, utterance or deed. Mahatma Gandhi considers non-violence to be eternal and natural. He rationalizes this thus:

"*Man is by nature nonviolent; otherwise, he could have destroyed himself before many centuries*".[1]

Non-violence is inherent in human nature and so he developed spirit of progress and mutual cooperation instead of destruction. He is in existence today owing to this factor. As such, non-violence is natural as well as eternal. It is our duty to gradually develop it and to tread on it in life of self.

If we ponder over the things with pure heart and impartially while keeping Gandhism apart, we shall really realize that violence never accorded anything. Contrary to that, non-violence has ever been welfaristic and whenever there has been a confrontation between violence and non-violence, it is non-violence that ultimately emerged victorious. The reason is clear. Non-violence is eternal. It is full of truth. Human life and lives of other beings - all depend upon it. It is permanently in human nature. It is because of it that a living being in last resort adopts non-violence. A being does not want that anyone should cause violence unto him or her. Each one loves life. All want to live. All escape death. It is, as such, that fundamental point of Gandhi's philosophy and views is non-violence.

Not only pertaining to 20th century; if we peruse history prior to this, we find that from time to time there have been confrontations and wars. Sometimes, the wars were very much dreadful and they continued not only for a year or two but also up to 20 or 25 years.

But, they could not give anything of permanent value to anyone. Ultimately, either the confronting parties were themselves tired and went into a treaty or the permanent spirit of non-violence in them made them realize the aptness of stopping belligerency. Some cherished a dream of temporary victory but in very near future, they were devoid of it. Right from the war between Sparta and Athens before Christ up to 2nd World War or up to all wars to date, above-mentioned fact is clear. Please try to study and you will find that my submission stands to be right.

GANDHISM & STATE OF CONFLICT:

After knowing that the root of Gandhism remains in non-violence and that it calls upon all to mutually cooperate along with opposing conflict, it is essential for us also to know as to how we can make our lives free from conflict through it. We should also know how to live a life of pleasure, prosperity and peace.

A human being has permanent as well as temporary tendencies. Consequently, in case there appears a state of cooperation as well as conflict in his behaviour, it is not a matter of surprise. It is for this reason that cooperation and confrontation have been termed to be compulsory in human society. However, we find everywhere that only those works ultimately become permanently successful which are done with spirit of cooperation. Contradictorily, the works done in a state of conflict are either unsuccessful or the success gained per them is quite temporary. Clearly, there is permanence in cooperation whereas a state of conflict remains, devoid of such an attribute. Co-operation earmarks non-violence; conflict cannot portray that. We may put it plainly that conflict symbolizes violence.

I have been immensely interested in History. I have studied history relating to whole world time to time right from ancient times to contemporary times. I have been in contact with many citizens of my country and of others and some of them can be said to be very much experienced. I have discussed things with them from time to time. Study of history, contacts and discourses; all these render my statement to be verified as truthful - the statement is - cooperation incorporates permanence and it symbolizes non-violence: in contradiction, conflict is temporary trait and it portrays violence. As far as question arises relating to my own experience, it also proves above-mentioned statement to be cent percent true. I have innumerable examples from my childhood, adolescence and age up to now and these all fully confirm the truthfulness of above-mentioned statement. I comprehend that there is no need of saying any more relating to this.

Many amongst you yourself are much experienced. You are learned also. Your learning relates to various spheres of life. You please peep into your life. I am firm on the opinion that you will find my conviction cent percent true about cooperation and conflict. Cooperation is a permanent trait and is fully affiliated with non-violence. Existence of every living being, not only of human being, depends upon it. Human progress or development is possible only by that. As such, it must be gradually awakened. As already mentioned, it is permanently present in nature. Cooperation and non-violence is one if affection and fraternity in cooperation happen to be strong.

Cooperation is permanent and natural as well. It is essential also. We can live our lives only through it. There is no sphere where it is not needed or happens to be insignificant. Let us take family that is first unit of human society. In case husband and wife and other members do not cooperate mutually in a family, it will perish. This is condition with society and nation also and what is true for a nation is also true in international context. The derivation is that cooperation is everywhere needed. In case it was not so, nice dictums like '*the universe is a family*', '*human unity*' or '*all offspring of a father*' could not have been uttered more than thousand years before. Propagators and great men of all religious communities could reiterate message of mutual cooperation only owing to that. All reiterated it because it is permanent and natural also. Many sacrificed selfish motives and struggled throughout life in order to accord a practical shape to it.

We have already illustrated that conflict is possible. If it takes place, its end is possible through the state of cooperation, which is nonviolent in essence. This is the message of Gandhism. In words of Mahatma Gandhi himself, "*Differences*[2] *cannot be finished by taking resort to violence*". In such state of affairs, whenever there is a state of conflict, it is foremostly important in accordance with Gandhian point of view that we must introspect. Through that, we must catch the basic point. The inference is to know the basic cause of that. Subsequently, we must give up that tendency which gives birth to the cause of conflict. When these two things are at hand, we must endeavour to resolve the conflict. A compromise after talks is the only solution. This is the best method, which incorporates liberality and forbearance. It is welfaristic to both parties. Through it both parties gain pleasant days of life.

If the two parties do not possess courage to resolve the state of conflict on their own, they must accept mediation of a third party. The third party should arrange a discourse and should get matured a compromise honestly and impartially. Subsequently, both belligerent parties must accept that compromise. It is another mode on which Gandhian philosophy lays emphasis. The first one is definitely better than the other. However, let it be second if we cannot get the 1st as this 2nd one also incorporates the state of cooperation.

If none of the two modes is accepted, the result will definitely be total doom. This doom is contradictory to human nature. As such, all should live with pleasure and prosperity, all should gain peace and must achieve their goal: this should be our motto. To gain this motto, we all have a duty to fulfill and that is to accept Gandhian message, which has its roots in non-violence. We should work towards gradual development of spirit of cooperation. We must have vow for this and should pass a resolution here at the end of 20th century even though it will really come to an end after about three years. This action of ours shall be written in golden letters in human history. We can now clearly grasp that a conflict leads only to inhumanity, non-progress and destruction. As such, we shall not allow repetition of all that which took place in the past, specifically, in 20th century. Gandhism expects this from you and me. This really happens to be the essence of Gandhism.

I want to shed the doubt regarding non-violence, which is at the root of Gandhism prior to ending my submission. A doubt is expressed that non-violence is a weapon of weak. It can be explained in the following manner- 'when there is non-capacity to combat, it is better to be 'non-violent'. Gandhism clearly combines bravery with non-violence. There is no place for weakness or cowardice in non-violent Gandhian philosophy. In case one says so - that is if one combines weakness or cowardice with non-violence, he does not know Gandhism. Gandhian principle consists of suffering with bravery, observing nonviolence while capable of violence and to oppose tyranny through this method. India's struggle for independence, which was carried out through non-violence under the leadership of Mahatma Gandhi, is the example.

Gandhism not only opposes injustice - in whatever form or coverage it may be - but also emphasizes its end through non-violence. Mahatma Gandhi's words are, "*We should not stoop before will of the oppressor...*"Contrary to it, one should accord one's whole spiritual power[3] against will of the atrocious.[4] Injustice should not be there in any form on any individual or group of individuals and nation or group of nations. If such a thing occurs, it is incumbent duty of each one, individual as well as nation, to work towards its end. It is responsibility of all to build a world based on non-violence that is cooperative spirit, ultimately finishing injustice.

Another significant thing is that there should be purity at heart while opposing injustice. If foremost status is accorded to selfish motive while doing so or the spirit of fulfilling selfish, motto remains supreme at any level, there will be abstinence of purity of heart. Non-violent Gandhian principle is violated wherever these nice norms are not accepted.

As such, we must develop spirit of cooperation from lower level to supreme level along with keeping selfishness apart. At this juncture, our strong will and spirit must be, in all ways, ready to 'sacrifice for eradication of injustice and getting justice. Today, when attempt is made to' finish the state of conflict when it appears, it either does not end immediately or it leaves a very bad impact. Sometimes, it takes very much time and it remains to be that any one of the belligerent parties or the 3rd party attempting to compromise betwixt them, remains involved in selfishness. The attempt towards finishing the conflict is not intrinsically made and there remains a spirit of fulfilling some selfish motive. There can be no solution in such a condition...As soon as selfishness is given up the condition becomes resolved because hearts become pure. It is on this accord Gandhism considers purity of heart to be essential for establishment of justice. There is full truthfulness in this Gandhian logic. World history up to today itself confirms that ultimately, purity of heart is also essential for non-violence. Cooperation is possible only when heart is pure.

The essence is that Gandhism gives a right to all to live with equality, pleasantly along with prosperity and peace. Its main basis is non-violence, which incorporates spirit of cooperation with all. It wants to end controversies and conflicts on this basis. This non-violence incorporates bravery. It accords lesson of sacrifice and calls upon to fully give up weakness or cowardice. It enunciates opposition of every sort of tyranny and demands justice for all. It also stipulates that giving up selfishness and adopting purity of heart are essential while doing so.

Let me and you all collectively derive inspiration from Gandhi and develop spirit of cooperation within us while giving non-violence unto our conduct. Along with that, we must aspire to bring whole human world within its sphere and should avoid conflicts. Time today demands this all very much from us.

References:

1. India of My Dreams, p. 84.
2. Differences of any plane: personal, family, community-related, social or even national-international.
3. While being non-violent.
4. Young India, 11th August 1920.

CHAPTER–9

RELEVANCE OF GANDHIAN NON-VIOLENCE IN THE MODERN POLITY

Presently a big portion of the world happens to be under Democratic system of Government. Theoretically, this system stands out to be the best up to now. This is a truth. It is the best because people: are connected with it directly or indirectly at every level. Not only this, it is this very system, which provides maximum opportunities of public progress and development. People can themselves decide in this system the mode of their welfare. However, even though being theoretically the best system of government, if we peruse the democratic nations, we first of all find that there is non-equal development of the citizens. We subsequently find that these nations are more or less victimized by regionalism. They have problem relating to language. They are under clutches of terrorism and communalism. There is also the problem of negation of human rights in these nations. There are other vivid problems akin to mention above and peace is far away so long as these problems exist. These nations should get themselves rid of these problems in toto, all citizens of them must have equal development and they should have communal harmony towards making all citizens collective and unified partners in progress. But, in reality, it is not so.

It is essential that the nations of democratic system of government should be free from above mentioned problems, must be capable of ensuring equal development of their all citizens and the citizens concerned must march forward on path of progress in unified way along with rendering contribution to world peace. Gandhian concept pertaining to non-violence is very much contextual today on this accord. It is significant. Let us grasp importance of Gandhism while analyzing it in brief.

GANDHISM:

In quite simple and clear words, Gandhism consists of the ideas, which Mahatma Gandhi put forth before human world. Along with that, to the maximum possible extent, Mahatma Gandhi treated his individual life in accordance with these ideas. Clearly, Gandhism is a mixture of Gandhi's concepts and practices. I do not hold merely his theory to be Gandhism. The basic groundship of Gandhism happens to be non-violence. This I have already stated at the beginning - at the time of proposal of a little amendment in the topic of the discourse. I have told about unification of Gandhism and non-violence. The non-violence is the most ancient eternal value. This non-violence is the ground of ancient-most civilization and culture of India. Mahatma Gandhi said on this very account while making his concepts and practices based on non-violence:

"*I have nothing new to teach you... Truth and-non-violence are as old as hill.*"

As we know, nonviolence and truth are two sides of the same coin. After knowing Gandhism, it is imperative for us to know clearly the concept of nonviolence also as it accords the ground for Gandhism.

NON-VIOLENCE:

What is non-violence? Ordinarily, we attribute non-violence as a dictum that prescribes non-snatching of anyone's life. Really, this is not complete derivation pertaining to the concept of non-violence. Non-violence is quite opposite to violence. As such, it would be better to know the position relating to violence in order to know non-violence and to be in knowledge of its meaning. According to a Jain scholar:

"*Whenever, we hurt some other living being through our thought, utterance or action under non-cordial stipulation and non-apt learning, such an impure spirit or act of destroying life of some other one, including the impure tendency, utterance or presuming, is taken to be full of vice of violence. In such a situation, even if there is no sort of violence externally, it intrinsically ipso facto remains a tendency of violence*".[1]

As a situation opposite to violence is non-violence, we can firmly state, "*Total non-violence consists in not hurting some other one's intellect, speech or action per own thought, utterance or deeds and not to deprive some one of his life*". We can clearly say this in a few words as follows: Abstinence in toto from violence is non-violence.

Mahatma Gandhi fully agrees with above-mentioned derivation of non-violence. He himself has said, "*Non-violence is not a concrete thing as it has generally been enunciated. Undoubtedly, it is a part of non-violence to abstain from hurting some living being but it is only an iota pertaining to its identity. The principle of nonviolence is shattered by every evil thought, false utterance, hate or wishing something bad unto some one. It is also shattered per possession of necessary worldly things*".[2] In this chain Mahatma Gandhi clarified in an edition of Young India:

"... *To hurt some one, to think of some evil unto some one or to snatch one's life under anger or selfishness, is violence. In contrast, purest non-violence is epitome in having a tendency and presuming towards spiritual or physical benefit unto every one without selfishness and with pure thought after cool and clear deliberations... The ultimate yardstick of violence or non-violence is the spirit behind the action*".[3]

Mahatma Gandhi, while in principle admitting his concept of non-violence, clarified further in this respect and said:

[A] NON-VIOLENCE IS PERPETUAL:

In context of non-violence being perpetual, Mahatma Gandhi states, "... *When we peruse the era from beginning unto now relating to the period for which we gain historical evidence, we find that man has been ultimately treading path of non-violence.*"[4] It is, as such, that non-violence came into existence along with man. In case it has not been with man from the very beginning, there might have been self-doom by man.[5]

However, it has not been that and not only human race is alive in such a huge number but there has been gradual enhancement in development and nearness in spite of presence of various obstacles and nuisances. This could never have been but because non-violence is perpetual, it happened.

[B] NON-VIOLENCE AND TRUTH BOTH ARE COMPLEMENTARY TO EACH OTHER:

Non-violence is governing because it is perpetual and permanent. It is on this accord that Mahatma Gandhi says, as I have already enunciated that "*Truth and Non-violence are two sides of the same coin. Both have same value. Difference consists in approach only. On one side there is non-violence, on other side is truth*".[6]

The derivation is that Truth stays with permanence or that Truth is permanent. Non-violence on account of being permanently present stays to be true.

[C] NON-VIOLENCE AND COWARDICE UNRELATED:

Mahatma Gandhi always believed in active non-violence. He always desisted inaction like a brave man. It is a truth relating to non-violence that it is not a weapon of a weak person. It has no place for cowardice. In own words of Mahatma Gandhi, "... *Non-violence should not be mistaken to be a true battle against every sort of evil*".[7] He further states:

"*In contrast, non-violence of my conception is true battle against evil, it is active confrontation and not a device of tit for tat.*"[8]

Mahatma Gandhi clarified to those who were keen to take non-violence to be a weapon of the weak or those who terming it as concrete and was upbringing non-action:

" ... *Non-violence and cowardice are not at all inter-related. I can think of a person to be coward at heart even if he is totally armed. In case it is not taken as cowardice to be equipped with arms, it is certainly symbolical of fearfulness. Pure non-violence is impossible without pure bravery*".[9]

He clearly said at innumerable occasions in time of national struggle for freedom that was being bravely carried out with fearlessness under his very leadership:

"...*Non-violence is an active force. There is no possibility of cowardice or weakness in it*".[10]

Further... "*There can be hope of a violent person being non-violent one day but there cannot be such a hope in relation to a coward*".[11]

[D] NON-VIOLENCE IS SOCIAL AS WELL:

Non-violence permanently exists in human nature and as I have stated, it came on earth with man. It can be said that one who is CREATOR of man on earth, is also ONE who kept non-violence permanently in human nature. Our existence could not have been if it was not so. We not only safeguarded our existence in its permanent presence but also progressed deeply and that is all clear before us. You are well aware that any progress is impossible without cooperation from others. When progress has been there, it is imperative that cooperation has been there. Cooperation is possible only when there is non-violence. As such, the non-violence, which is individually present, remains present socially also. It is in this accordance that Mahatma Gandhi says:

"*...Nonviolence is not only individualistic, it is social* also".[12]

Logically, he further states in this regard :

"*It must be developed. We are bound to admit that regulation of mutual relations in society is through non-violence to a considerable extent. I wish it to be developed on large scale*".[13]

To those who take non-violence to be merely an individual notion, he said without mincing words, "*It is not true that society cannot be organized or operated on basis of non-violence. I oppose such a statement*".[14]

[E] NON-VIOLENCE IS ALL-TIMELY & ALL WELFARISTIC:

As I have said, non-violence emerged on earth with man and Mahatma Gandhi took it to be perpetual and eternal. In this chain, he called upon the people to continue to develop it in practice throughout life while taking non-violence to be the basis of life. He said, "*Non violence should not be practiced on specific occasion only*".[15] It is well timely. It is not short-lived or casual. Along with this, Mahatma Gandhi admits non-violence along with dogma of all-welfare and equality in toto. He separates it from utilitarianism completely and instantly from this point of view. In his own words:

"*A worshipper of non-violence cannot ditto utilitarianism. He will work towards 'Sarvabhoothitaya' that is maximum benefit of all and shall perish himself while constantly endeavouring to gain the ideal. Maximum pleasure of all includes maximum pleasure of maximum number also. Follower of non-violence and utilitarianism will be found so many times at a path but ultimately an occasion will be there when they will find themselves forced to tread separate paths. In certain directions, they will also have to oppose each other. A utilitarian cannot sacrifice himself for the sake of saving his argumentation whereas a non-violent is always ready to face perishment*".[16]

[F] GODLY FAITH IS ESSENTIAL FOR NON-VIOLENCE:

Mahatma Gandhi integrally combines non-violence with God. According to him, "*It is impossible to tread path of 'Truth and Non violence' unless one has vital faith in God. God is that alive force which incorporates all remaining forces of the world. This force does not depend upon anyone and it exists even when all other forces in world come to an end. In case I do not believe unto this all glittering light, that incorporates everything, I fail to understand as to how am I alive*".[17]

God is really the Lord of universe. He accorded non-violence on earth along with man so that man can progress along with his existence and gain ambition. God kept all within the region of equality along with, that. He has no consideration towards discrimination all small or big, high or low, rich or poor etcetera. It is possible only through developing, nonviolence that a man attempts to tread his life while practicing these non-discriminations in life. When man does so, he cannot at all ignore God who happens to be the Lord and who kept non-violence permanently in his nature.

These are, some significant clarifications, which Mahatma Gandhi offers in context of non-violence. No doubt, non-violence is natural, true, and perpetual and a device that is far away from cowardice. It is social value also along with being an individualistic one; it is all-timely and all welfaristic also. It is essential to believe in God if one cherishes to believe and practice non-violence. When I myself ponder over, I firmly believe that all eternal values get themselves comprehended unto nonviolence. Forbearance can be there only while non-violence is in existence. Unity, compassion, fraternity, justice or equality is also for its help alone. It is basis, mother and up bringer of all the values.

MAHATMA GANDHI, NON-VIOLENCE AND DEMOCRACY:

While accepting dictum of all-welfare as basis and not that of majority[18], Mahatma Gandhi is certainly a staunch supporter of democracy and along with that, he wants that it should be intermingled with nonviolence in every manner. In such a democracy, "*Quantum of interference in liberty of people happens to be minimum*".[19]

In fact, Mahatma Gandhi takes real democracy to be that admits governmental interference at the minimum, which has peace at the maximum and all progress on the basis of equality. It is possible only when non-violence is imparted the supreme status in practice as well as in principle and at social as well as individual plane. Only such a democracy can be successful in its real goal.

We could know the derivation pertaining to non-violence and also by perusing Gandhian point of view, its significance for human race. We could clearly know that it is only non-violence, which can make life prosperous at every level. When it is so why should not the democratic countries make themselves prone to non-violence in the event that these countries with democratic governance system accept welfare of all citizens to be their ambition or goal? Mahatma Gandhi wants this very all out of the system of government and it is really a thing of significance. It is such a significant matter that this reality cannot be denied by me or by anyone amongst you. It is on this accord that Gandhian nonviolence is immensely significant in system of today's governance, especially in a democratic system.

Presently, the democratic system in operation in worldly nations is not according to Gandhian principle. We are not getting what Mahatma Gandhi ultimately cherished from democracy. If it was so, these nations could be devoid of atmosphere of violence and presence of fear.[20]

There could not have been corruption and divided human society. I have already emphasized that there could not have been problems pertaining to terrorism, communalism, regionalism and relating to languages. More than this all, there could not have been observance of ethical and moral degradation in public life. Such degradation is being observed constantly. The main cause after all these things remain that all activities of these nations are not non-violent. There cannot be any possibility of violence while there is Gandhism in democracy. Violence is not sacred, pure or welfaristic from any point of view. Whatever is gained on basis of it is impure and temporary. It is on this accord that it cannot pace with democracy even for a moment. Mahatma Gandhi says, "*Democracy and violence can never be mutual*".[21]

Basis of democracy is non-violence in toto. And, there cannot be any diminution in it. Non-violence should be real; not merely titular. Democracy shall be pro-people only while so. Mahatma Gandhi said in this context, "*If they are to be truly made democratic, they must be valiantly non-violent.*"[22] In case of absence of this attribute, democracy shall be there for name sake only and it would be better for it to... clearly be supporter of dictatorship.[23]

MODERN SYSTEM OF GOVERNANCE AND NON-VIOLENT GANDHIAN WAY:

After above-mentioned analysis, the question arises before us as to how to guide modem system of government, especially democracy, towards Gandhian way, which undoubtedly has non-violence as its basic root. Then, it is to be made and quotable towards equal development of all citizens. This democracy must be such that "it should not warrant power of punishment."[24]

In it, "... *people will certainly be conscious regarding their duties: they may sometimes, of course, be ignorant towards their rights.*"[25]

In case there is something anti-people in it, the people shall make it favourable to them per non-violent means.

As we have analyzed, Mahatma Gandhi is in favour of spontaneous development of non-violence. To make democracy ultimately in accordance with non-violence remains to be his goal. This is possible. He rightly said in this regard, "... *Non-violence is not merely an individual concept. It is social concept also. It must be developed in this form.*"[26]

Development is essential and it is in sight. He again states in this regard along with citing a nice example, "*Mutual practices in society are regulated by non-violence to a considerable extent. I want it to be at development at larger scale.*"[27]

This should of course, be done in right direction and with truthful spirit.

It is the inference that the non-violence permanently present in human nature should be developed in practice from its present state towards progressive one in right direction per truthful spirit. A true and cherished democracy shall be established only in such a condition. A system shall be commendable in proportion to non-violence in it. This is important regarding every system, however, the government of the people-democracy - remains foremost in this chain. We have accordingly assigned it topmost place under our discourse.

Polity must be fearless, full of equality, providing protection to all eternal values and only then it can be pro-people. It can accord apt dimension to development. Man can contribute to world peace only in such a system of government along with gaining his goal. Government should be welfaristic to people and above being non-violent as enunciated by Mahatma Gandhi. Gandhian principle of non-violence is very much significant in modern system of government from this point of view. This significance is likely to be of permanent nature perpetually.

THE DEMOCRACY OF MAHATMA GANDHI'S IMAGINATION:

Yes, the democracy of Mahatma Gandhi's imagination - fully encircled with non-violence - exists in no nation of the world as up to now. Democracy of his imagination happens to be one, which does not have any provision of punishment and even an organization like State happens to be obsolete in it. This is because Mahatma Gandhi holds, "*...State is symbolical of centralized and organized violence.*"[28]

As nonviolence is connected with human soul, man can be non-violent whereas in opposition to it:

"*...State is a soul-less machine. On this accord, it is impossible to get rid of violence. Its very existence depends upon violence.*"[29]

Non-existence of state as cherished by Mahatma Gandhi is impossible instantly or in near future. Even then, it is incumbent on the people, who are living in state organizations, to develop non-violence that is permanently present in their nature and to enhance it gradually up to adequate level. Along with that, all systems [specifically democracy] should, work in direction of development of non-violence at individual, community, social and national levels. The atmosphere of fear which we see, the diminution of values in life and the problems having cropped up vividly cannot be eradicated without developing it.

There is no alternative to non-violence. The whole human history is within our purview. Whenever polities were under clutches of violence, tacitly or expressively, they could not get anything except doom and disaster to their citizens. Their own peace was fully shattered per this doom and others were also badly affected. It is in this regard that in accordance with philosophy of Mahatma Gandhi, non-violence should be admitted as invariable part of our life and it is on the basis of this dictum that modern polities must operate. This will be very nice for them.

I have stated that these polities cannot all of a sudden operate as per expectation of the Great Mahatma Gandhi. Non-violence cannot be a part of conduct instantly, but Mahatma Gandhi's suggestion is very important in this regard[30] as I have already mentioned. However, the polities must forward certainly in this direction. Needless to say that non-violence is true, natural, enemy of fearfulness, stands at top amongst eternal values including the equality and has been gradually progressive. Its nice and vital example is before us in the form of its development unto today, since the inception of human race - that is since initial human - state. We clearly see that in spite of differences to whatsoever extent, ultimately there is an innovative desire for peace. This is because non-violence happens to be in human nature, as I have said again and gain, and human being like it.

Gandhism calls upon modem polities to march in this direction and to make them prone to non-violence. This is really welfaristic. We cannot at all minimize significance of Gandhian non-violence in modem polity.

References:

1. *Jain Darshan* ... Page 321.
2. *Mangal Prabhat*, 1945, p. 7.
3. Young India, Ahmedabad, October 4, 1928.
4. *Harijan Sevak*, August 11, 1940, p. 219.
5. Young India, January 2, 1930.
6. *Harijan Sevak*, July 13, 1947.
7. Young India, Ahmedabad, June 4, 1925.
8. Same as above.
9. *Harijan*, July 15, 1939.
10. Young India, June 16, 1927.
11. Same as above.
12. *Harijan*, July I, 1939.
13. Same as above.
14. As above, December 3, 1938.
15. *Harijan*, September 5, 1936.
16. *Sarvodaya*, 1955 p. 4 and Hindi *Navjivan*, December I, 1926.
17. *Harijan Sevak*, July 28, 1946.
18. Mahatma Gandhi clearly told in 2nd March, 1922 edition of Young India "I*t is slavery to accept every decision of majority. Democracy is not an epitome in which people should behave like sheep. Liberty of man's thoughts and actions is cautiously guarded in democracy.*"
19. *Harijan*, January II, 1936.
20. The nations having democratic system are practically the victims of difficulties and problems even though they are committed to total and equal progress of their citizens. People in general are not fearless and their life is far away from peace.

21. Harijan Sevak, November 12, 1938.
22. Same as above.
23. As above.
24. The Epic Fast, 1932, p. 102.
25. Harijan, March 15, 1938 and Harijan, July 6, 1947 in which he wrote, "*If instead of insisting on rights everyone does his duty, there will be the rule of order established among mankind. There is no such thing as the divine right of kings to rule and the humble duty of the ryots to pay respectful obedience to their masters.*" [See appendix-B for more details of Mahatma Gandhi's article written in *Harijan* on 06-07-1947 under the title 'Rights or Duties]
26. Same as above, January 7, 1939.
27. *Harijan*, January 7, 1939.
28. Modem Review, 1935, p. 412.
29. Same as above.
30. Mahatma Gandhi says, "*My opinion rests on my belief in the infinite possibilities of the individual to develop non-violence. The more you develop it in your own being, the more infectious it becomes, till it overwhelms your surroundings and by and by might over sweep the world.*" [Mahatma - D.G. Tendulkar, Vol. 5 1952, p. 14]

❑❑❑

CHAPTER–10

GANDHI'S LEGACY AND NUCLEARISED STATES OF SOUTH ASIA

A person in accordance with his viewpoint makes the estimated value or assessment of a scholar or a great man, or a philosopher. I have my own conception pertaining the life and work of Mahatma Gandhi. Not only in respect of one or two but also of his numerous ideologies, I do not concur, for example, Gandhi accepted Hindu Varna System as Godly and even stated:

"*In Varna System only, the four fold creation of society appears to me real, Godly and essential*".[1]

I do not fully agree with this viewpoint. In my view, it never remained in that shape as it is presented in ideal form.

Mahatma Gandhi has accepted several mythological traditions. I may not accept them. I also do not completely fall in with him in respect of woman education. I truly and explicitly narrate my disagreement with the various ideologies of Gandhi. Simultaneously, I am the favourite and admirer of Gandhi from the core of my heart for the legacy he has left for the welfare of the generations to come by his steadfast principles and attitude. Certainly at the basis of legacy, there is '*Ahimsa*' [non-violence]. There is no place in it even for the smallest weapon. To talk of Atom Bomb, is the greatest sin. One, who talks of weapon, goes miles away from Gandhian legacy and anyone keeping Atom Bomb or supporting it, and talks of Gandhi or Gandhism will be doing a great sin to the human society as a whole.

This principally scrupulous and practical legacy of Gandhi is not limited up to South Asia or India. It is meant for the whole world. He awakened the whole of mankind. The scope of his thinking was not only India or South Asia but it was the entire humanity. It is another thing: that whatever he did practically, besides South Africa, remained mostly confined to India.

Now it is quite natural for you to ask what is the theory and practice of Mahatma Gandhi, which I have already described as his legacy. In this context, I will once again reiterate my conviction, which I narrated while starting the subject. I said that a person according to his viewpoint makes the assessment of any scholar, great man or philosopher. I too have my own conception about Mahatma Gandhi. I believe the very truth about his theory and practice, which I have named as his legacy in this context. Many scholars assess the theory and practice of Gandhi superlatively. I do not claim to assess according to them. While making assessment when scholars proceed towards conclusion, they do not hold identical views of their own. Some one believes in a particular portion of his theory and practice as his legacy while another one in his other portion. Some one differs from the two. It is their right to assess in their own way. I have no objection to that. However, it is very well known to me that the theory and practice of Mahatma Gandhi, is within the circle of non-violence. Whatever any one deduces if it is within the scope of non-violence, certainly it is Gandhism.

If anyone says that Mahatma Gandhi talks of equality, so the portion of equality in his theory and practice, is his legacy, I will certainly accept it. Why so? It is because no equality is possible in the absence of non-violence. Equality is the complement of non-violence. Similarly, if anyone says that Mahatma Gandhi stresses more on freedom and this only is his legacy, I shall also agree to it.

Dwelling in state of freedom and definitely believing the same for others as well is the true interpretation of freedom. It is not possible without non-violence. Therefore, the people accepting Mahatma Gandhi's view pertaining to freedom or the work done by him in this context, as his legacy, are also just and right.

Mahatma Gandhi has stated not to bend before injustice. This is to say he invokes and stresses on justice. For the establishment of justice, he struggled several times. So if certain friends call his invocation of establishment of justice as his legacy, it will not be improper. True or real justice can only be feasible when non-violence is at its roots. Certain renowned Gandhian call Mahatma's concept of '*SARVODAYA*' as his legacy for the future generations. In *Sarvodaya*, there is the desire for welfare of all from the lowest level. In it there is not the idea of benefit for the maximum number, if the welfare of all is the idea, it is possible only in a state of non-violence. So people believing in the *Sarvodaya* of Mahatma as his legacy are true and just in their own way.

In the same way unity, love, friendship, truthfulness etc., as immortal values, can be cohesively integrated with the theory and practical legacy of Mahatma Gandhi. They all come within the scope of non-violence. So the people assessing in this aspect, are more or less correct in their stand. Ultimately, non-violence is the root. No one can ever venture to separate non-violence from the legacy of Gandhi.

Despite all this what I deem and assert as the most important part of Gandhi's theory and practice, as his legacy for the future generations, it is Harmony, It is particularly important because in day to day individual, family, community, social, national or international dealings, Harmony occupies a dominant position.

Harmony is complementary to all other values viz. unity, love, friendship, truthfulness, equality, liberty or *Sarvodaya*. And it is completely and cohesively integrated with non-violence. It is also owing to the fact that Mahatma Gandhi not only gave an important place to it in his philosophy but also practically worked for it for the whole of his life. Whatever success he achieved in South Africa, and thereafter in India; was all due to creating Harmony among the people. Even he sacrificed his life in an attempt to maintain it. Even today there is imperative need of Harmony for the existence of all of us, for our progress and for peace.

You may probe into the word meaning of Harmony, you may define it in any way, you may interpret it in any form, you have full right to do so, Even then, I think the main spirit behind HARMONY is '*Purity of Heart*'. This purity of heart begets Harmony. Till there is purity of heart, man naturally thinks of Harmony and acts accordingly, By thinking and acting as such, he has knowledge that in others' welfare, his own welfare is also included. At that time, he is cautious. But it is, universally known that in worldly affairs, man, generally becomes subjected to indifferent attitude. You may attach any reason for the same. Consequently, he becomes indifferent to Purity of Heart, When Purity of Heart is absent in him, he ceases to think of' Harmony or to do any work for the restoration of the same. Along with it, he stage by stage, more or less, also becomes the cause of downfall. So, for the welfare at every level; maintenance of Harmony is: imperative. If this does not happen, then certainly man fixes the question mark as to his own existence.

I have said that Harmony is complement of all immortal values. Simultaneously, it is the integral part of non-violence. And because, it is most essential and essential too in day-to-day practices, Mahatma Gandhi up to the last moment of his life worked for it, in theory and practice. In this connection he had been laying stress on three aspects:

- To honour the will of others;

- To make continuous progress in the increase of friendship; and
- To imbibe soul patience with devotion.

While stressing upon the above aspects, which are really humane, Mahatma Gandhi gave many suggestions. Not only personal or relating to family but also pertaining to community, at social, national and international level. He inspired to work for the same. For example, in this series, he considered the education of harmony as compulsory part of Syllabus; He expressed hope that the educational institutions will work for Harmony. By doing so, they will be able to fulfill their aim.

So far as the personal life of Mahatma Gandhi is concerned, is certainly the unique example of Harmony, which is also imitable. In this connection, many such instances can be cited, which can give you surprise. Perhaps you know that for about thirty years, Mahatma Gandhi led the Indians against British Empire to liberate India. But while doing all this, Mahatma Gandhi never separated Harmony from his person. In this context, he got justice, while keeping Harmony in every condition. It is the beautiful and wonderful example before the world. Side by side, it is fully humane, and beneficial. Generally, we find that in the state of struggle to maintain Harmony is not an easy task. But it is also equally true that Mahatma Gandhi continued to maintain it.

Whenever he came to know that there was danger to Harmony in a particular community or at a particular place, he girded up the loins and started his work and did not return from that place and community till he re-established the atmosphere of perfect harmony over there. In this respect we can cite many world famous instances.

What is that which is not possible in the atmosphere of Harmony? I am firmly of the belief that all which is within the manly strength and access can certainly be achieved in harmonious condition. There occurs lack of care and caution. With the result bitterness or animosity prevails. If the condition worsens more, it leads to dispute. Further confrontation or war may also be ignited. But purity of heart, which is the progeny of Harmony, bringing all differences, strives and wars to extinction may enable us to have a glimpse of such a happy morning, which is pleasurable and full of welfare for one and all. So Mahatma Gandhi stresses more on this by practicing it on himself. So I accept this Harmony as the most conspicuous legacy of Mahatma Gandhi for future generations. It is also the call of time. As I have already stated it is connected with non-violence.

I have appealed and stressed that the legacy of Mahatma Gandhi is meant for the whole world. It would certainly be unjust to confine it exclusively to South Asia or India. Mahatma Gandhi was the greatest humanist of his time. Whatever he said and did was for the entire human society and is yet and will ever remain so. Yes, it is true that he mostly experimented his theory in India. The world is so vast. No great man, or even a messenger of God can make the whole world as the place of his practices or activities. '*Karma-bhoomi*', can only be a particular place or nation. However, the message of that '*Karma*' can be disseminated allover the world.

When Atom bombs were dropped on 'Hiroshima' and 'Nagasaki', Mahatma said, "*Atomic weapons can never be checked by other atomic weapons*". He called it as 'the severest, formidable and inhuman act and invoked for the total abandonment of all the atomic weapons'. But unfortunately at that time, nations having nuclear weapons or capabilities and even others did not take this inhuman act seriously. Billions and millions of Dollars or Pounds were spent on the manufacture of atomic weapons, turning the face away from the crores of people, starving, necked, deprived of habitation, medicinal treatment and education. Consequently the horrible plight that assumed subsequently is well before us.

More distressing subject is that even the nations of South Asia have stepped in this direction. Much ignorant and indifferent from the reality and horrible consequences, these nations, it appears, have ceased to honour the will of others knowingly or unknowingly. Instead of developing friendship and fraternity, they have probably preferred the atmosphere of dreadful arm manufacturing competition and increasing tension and animosity. They lack patience. They have now hardly any devotion and respect for the path shown and treaded by apostles of peace among whom' Mahatma Gandhi also occupies his unique position. There appears less of inclination towards purity of heart, the offshoot of Harmony. They have gone far away from it and become much aloof from the legacy of Gandhi.

I again reiterate, if there is purity of heart, there can be no dispute that cannot be solved. If there is the idea of Harmony in the mind and every function in life is performed in accordance with then everything can be achieved in life? Contrary to this, in the absence of purity of heart and Harmony, you may manufacture any sort of dreadful weapons, create an atmosphere of terror by atomic experiments, you will not be able to achieve anything in life. Yes, you will be losing so many things important for running the life from personal level to international sphere; and are yet constantly suffering and losing. It is a bare fact and truth.

My friend Dr. Anand, working for peace, at the time of inviting me to negotiate with you, had requested me, to speak particularly about South Asia., I have a great regard for Dr. Anand. I want to say to Anand that I am in the habit of plain speaking from my childhood. Sometimes I have crossed the limits of plain speaking. So I became the victim of incurring displeasure of father, family and the nearest and dearest ones. Not only this, I was also given a sound beating for this attitude of mine. Thereafter, in my community, society and country many became my opponent. I have love for all. All are mine own. But what can I do? I cannot follow the path of untruth. So I cannot turn my face away from reality. Now if someone is displeased with me, becomes my opponent, even then I shall tread on the way, 1 have chosen for myself.

I have also said very plainly today. The nations of South Asia appear to have gone astray from Mahatma Gandhi's legacy. The harmony for which Gandhi sacrificed his life, these nations are advancing towards opposite direction. If they bring even the least the truth and reality of life in their mind, they will come to know of the reality of life. 50 percent people of these nations are living below poverty line. And as I have said, earlier, this population stands in deprivation of basic human needs. Gandhi wants *SARVODAYA* through Harmony. Then there is no need of any arm and ammunition. But what is this? Here the weapons are atomic. Certainly it is dishonour to Mahatma's legacy.

I can determinedly assert that the nations of South Asia nave been competitively engaged -in mad race of dreadful weapons for the last fifty years. Some of them have gained nuclear capability. Even then their problems, more or less, remain as they have ever been. These problems are both internal and external. Now if these nations adopt the harmonious legacy of Mahatma Gandhi for twenty five years, adopt and follow the concept of honouring the will of others', spirit of 'friendship and fraternity, simultaneously, imbibe soul patience and devotion to one and all, certainly they will liberate themselves and get rid of all their standing problems. Side by side, convey such a pious message to the world at large wherein there lies complete welfare of mankind.

Reference:

1. Young India, Ahmedabad, 8 December 1920.

□□□

CHAPTER–11

GANDHISM, PEACE EDUCATION AND CONSTRUCTION OF SUSTAINABLE CULTURE OF PEACE

Gandhism, an abridged form or amalgam of Mahatma Gandhi's views and practices, revolves around non-violence-a great human value that is permanently present in the nature and always welfaristic. Non-violence, besides being an essential condition for the existence, is the basis of development and the achievement of a considered goal. What is the goal? Of course it is PEACE. That's why emphasis has been laid on the continuing awakening and adoption of non-violence individually and collectively in day-to-day practices. In other words, efforts have been afoot for the construction of a culture accepting non-violence to be the fundamental point so that the existence of mankind is assured,[1] the path of development is smoothened and the ultimate goal of peace is well within sight and approach. There is no let-up in these endeavours and this process shall continue with the same gusto in future as well.

History of mankind is very old running into million of years. This history has been divided into different ages and it is an undeniable fact that education has played a very vital role and has consequently made a sizeable contribution in awakening of non-violence and its adoption in daily practices, what so ever method may have been adopted with the changed times. It was necessary too. Education in its real meanings is "*SA VIDYAYA VIMUKTAYE*". In this chain in 20eth century, Mahatma Gandhi made a momentous contribution showing a justifiable, simple and wonderful way for awakening and adoption of non-violence in the routine chores of life. For this, he, right from the beginning, considered non-violence to be an indivisible, important and essential part of education and fixed the responsibility of each and every concerned individual whether parents, teachers, leaders of society or students. He did so that every human being living on this planet was assured of safe and secure life, without any fear and equally marching towards development, having peace; strengthening the culture of peace.

Gandhism, its system of education, which, in fact, is the education of peace, according to Mahatma Gandhi, "----*is an unending exercise till death divides into different stages* ---" It is undoubtedly, ever relevant to global- Peace or for the construction of a real sustainable culture of peace, specially under a democratic set-up. In this context the necessity of its relevance and importance of its role can never be underrated/minimized. The need of the day is to understand Gandhism well and to put it into practice in the process of education world over.

Reference:

1. This concept, according to Mahatma Gandhi, is based upon an intensive research by Rishis thousands years ago. In Mahatma Gandhi's words, "*The Rishis, who discovered the law of non-violence in the midst of violence, were greater geniuses than Newton. They were themselves greater warriors than Wellington. Having themselves known the use of arms they realized their uselessness, and taught a weary world that its salvation lay not through violence but through non-violence.* Non-violence in a dynamic condition means conscious..." In this context he urged further, "*I want India to practise non-violence being conscious of her strength and power. No training in arms is required for realization of her strength. We seem to need it, because we seem to think that we are but a lump of flesh. I want India to recognize that she has a soul that cannot perish and that can rise triumphant above every physical weakness and defy the physical combination of the whole world.*"

□□□

CHAPTER–12

ON PROBLEM OF COMMUNALISM

Communalism is one of the most serious problems that India has to face after her freedom from colonial rule in the mid of 20eth Century. This problem, which has existed among the followers of two principal religious communities Hindus and Muslims - many times raised a great challenge before the secular structure of India. In the name of religion such acts have been committed that are no doubt shameful and a act of fleeing from the message of Mahatma Gandhi who lead the country to the door steps of freedom through non-violence, the sacred human value.

Mahatma Gandhi devoted his entire life for propounding communal harmony. He whished in 'India of his dream', "*I shall for an India, in which the poorest shall feel that it is their country in whose making they have an effective voice; an India in which there shall be no high class and low class of people; [and above all] an India in which all communities shall live in perfect harmony.*"

But it is unfortunate that after independence to this year, i.e. up to the year 2002, there have been over five thousand communal riots in India, and most of them occurred between Hindus and Muslims. After all, why have there been riots in such a large number? In other words, what is the reason for them? Whether is it one reason or are there many reasons? What is the impact of such riots on common man? What situation is created at national-international level due to these riots? These are the questions you become curious to get an answer to. Along with this you would want to know, how to get rid of this problem. Come let us try to find answers to these questions pertaining to the problem of communalism in India. But prior to it, let us know and understand the meaning and definition of communalism.

Not only in India but also all over the world, scholars and subject-specialists have defined communalism in different ways. And, all these definitions, unfortunately, do not reveal the complete meaning or sense of communalism in clear-cut terms. However, Richard C. Lambert, who has given the definition of community according to the conditions prevailing in the country, provides us a correct picture regarding the position of communalism in India.

According to Richard C. Lambert, "*The word Community is used in India for the unequal social units.*" It may be said that communalism is the negative aspect of the community. That is to say, when the people of a particular community care only for their own narrowly concerned interests, through the means of their religious faiths, old customs and conservative practices, disregarding the interests of whole society, then it may be termed as communalism.

In general, following four main things can be found in a state of communalism:

- Negativeness;
- Narrowness;
- Unfair means; and
- Disregard to the interests of society.

The unfair means that are adopted in a state of communalism, neglecting the interests of society, instigation on the basis of religious sentiments is the main among them, which can be observed clearly in communal violence that occurred during the last 55 years in India.

II

India has a history of communal riots. The problem of communalism, especially relating to the modern age, and seeds of which were sown during the 19th century, is a gift of colonial rulers to India. In other words, the colonialists played the main role in starting communal tension in India in the 19th Century. Along with this, some people from a particular religious community were also involved in this act, who keeping aside the interests of entire Indian Society and filled with narrow-minded thoughts, joined hands with the colonialists. They were also in favour of bargaining with the colonialists for the benefit of their co-religionists. It was an easy task for them. India is a country of diversities, a land of different religious communities and sects. In such a country, if the government protects the people of a particular community who are ready to fulfill their own interest even by spreading communalism, what can be difficulty for them? They can do so without any fear.

Towards the end of the19th century, Bal Gangadhar Tilak, who was one of the great political leaders of India at that time, started "*Ganesh Pooja*" and "*Shivaji Mahotsav*" in Southern India, especially in Maharashtra and its nearby regions, with the aim of creating awakening among the masses. I hope, even today, nobody can believe that while starting "*Ganesh Pooja*" or "*Shivaji Mahotsav*" programmes, would have contemplated about Hindu-Muslim, or there would be any thought in his mind in the interest of Hindus - his co-religionists. He was one who always thought and worked for Indians, Indian nation and Indian nationalism. The programmes related to "*Ganesh Pooja*" and "*Shivaji Mahotsav*" was not initiated to support the interests of Hindus. However, both "*Ganesh*" and "*Shivaji*" were associated with the emotions of a number of Hindus.

A procession connected with the above programme was passing through the streets of Mumbai in the year 1893. When it reached near a place of prayer of another religious community, it was pelted with stones. The quarrel ensued between those participating in the procession and attackers, and finally resulted in a communal riot. Similarly, another incident occurred in the coming year, i.e. in 1894 at Pune. Behind both these incidents was the support of colonial rulers to the narrow-minded people involved in the acts.

From here, started communalism, which was also evident on some occasions in the Gandhian era of the national liberation movement of India. Mahatma Gandhi, as I have already said, was committed to communal harmony. He was of the firm belief that if the followers of two principal religious communities - Hindu and Muslim walk hand in hand, come forward together to solve the problems, small or big: become identical to nationalism, only then the progress of the country will be possible in real sense and the cultural heritage of India will be protected.

According to his firm belief, Mahatma Gandhi entered in the "*Yajna*" of national freedom along with others, whether they were Sikhs or Buddhists, Parsis or Jains, Christians or Muslims, or his own co-religionists. He, as all know, accepted *ahimsa* as both, means and goal. He made it the basis for achieving freedom for India. In my opinion, *ahimsa* holds due place in all religious communities. I do not believe that it does not help the followers of any community to perform his or her duty. Rather I believe that it is *ahimsa* alone that assists to enable us to fulfill our duties in the best possible manner.

But it was unfortunate that many people could not become identical with the firm and true message of Mahatma Gandhi pertaining to non-violence. Even then, he, time and again, repeated his message of *ahimsa* till the last breath of his life; worked for communal harmony declaring it a value supplementary to non-violence. He, time and again, conveyed suggestions for peace brigades[1] and for volunteers[2] to work for harmony. These suggestions are more or less important even today for a country like India.

III

After independence there came a change in social, political and economic conditions of India, which was quite natural. There were many reasons for change in social conditions such as: the provision of equality before law, equal opportunities to all to get job etc., and above all, liberalization of the ownership of land. The change in political conditions mainly depended on adopting a democratic system for which all adults [men and women] of the country got the right to choose their representatives. Similarly, there was a definite change in the economic conditions as well. The freedom of earning livelihood by fair means, without any fear or pressure, was given to everyone. And, all rich or poor, so-called high or low, became entitled to government jobs without any distinction. All these things were truly symbolic of change in economic conditions.

With these unprecedented changes, the best atmosphere of communal harmony should have been created in India and according to the expectation of Mahatma Gandhi this country should have become an example in this direction. But this did not happen. Then, what happened? The same I have mentioned in the beginning. Communalism has become a serious problem in India and it has greatly damaged the country. After independence, there have been many reasons behind this problem. Along with this, it has also undergone numerous changes. Besides two religious communities, two sects of the same community, or even between sub-sects, you can see the atmosphere of conflicts. Even then, most of the problems of communalism in India revolve around Hindus and Muslims, which is a matter of great concern.

In my opinion the reasons for the problem of communalism in India are mainly two - silent and apparent. Side by side, there is also a third different reason that can be observed in several other countries of the world.

The reasons, which I have termed as silent, must be analyzed very carefully in relation to the problem of communalism in India. Among these reasons is the large number of unemployed youths that comprise nearly ten per cent of the total population, i.e. ten crores; illiteracy and poverty is the main. Perhaps, you know that there are twenty-five provinces and seven union territories in India. In some of these provinces, even after fifty-five years of independence, fifty or even more percent people are illiterate. Also in the entire country 26 per cent people live below the poverty line.

Poverty, illiteracy and unemployment create a lot of compulsions, especially before younger generation. That is why, many from younger generation, because of lack of right thinking, remain unemployed and in a state of poverty, get involved in the evil like communalism. In this context, as I have already mentioned, a minute and careful analysis is necessary. After this analysis certain remedial steps must be taken. The efforts being made for uprooting poverty, illiteracy and unemployment are not as fruitful as they should be.

With reference to communalism whatever apparent reasons are discussed generally, among them the first one is religious, and the second one is political. Third one is socio-economic and the fourth one is international. In the first, i.e. religious, its fundamentalism should be considered responsible for communalism. Malevolence like reactionary attitude, traditional bourgeois and conservative approaches etc. are mainly behind fundamentalism.

After all 'Our belief alone is true' and 'rest is untrue or incomplete', we find this kind of mentality of fundamentalists. As per this mentality, when the followers of any religious community, sect or sub-sect indulge in their activities, they certainly come in conflict with others. Reason is quite evident. They do not have tolerance, which is absolutely neccessary for a country like India - a land of different religious communities. They become the cause of confrontation, malice and struggle.

Politicians also have played a villainous role in creating serious communal situations in India. There was politics at the root of painful division of India in 1947 in the name of a particular religious community. But even after paying a heavy price in the form of partition, in many riots provoked thereafter, we can find the involvement directly or indirectly, of political parties or their supporters. Along with this for the sake of vote bank, the policy of appeasement, selection of candidates on the basis of community, sect, sub-sect and caste, and flaring up religious sentiments at the time of elections, led to the rise of communalism. These practices are still continued and the country is bearing heavy loss because of it. We can witness many adverse results of these practices.

Economic and social reasons can be found mainly in competition among the people living at lower and lower-medium levels and in the involvement of professional hooligans, speculators and the anti-social elements in communal riots. This involvement is, purely for economic gains and to attain overwhelming influence on society. I find the above said realities and reasons in riots occurred a few years back in my own city and also in other cities like Mumbai.

External elements also have a role in worsening the problem of communalism, and making it serious. I may not mention the name of any particular country in this regard but scholars and those who think on this problem from time to time are quite aware of this fact.

The main reasons for involvement of external elements or their role in riots are as follows:

- To create an atmosphere of instability, so that it becomes socially weak;
- To hope for gaining sympathy from minorities;
- To try to weaken the economic structure of a foreign country; and
- With the aim to conceal their own incompetence.

Besides above-mentioned facts there can be more - silent or apparent - reasons in all areas, which create communalism or enhance it, or make it serious. There are also some such reasons that rise instantaneously and result in communal disturbances or in riots of serious nature.

Other than silent and apparent, the third reason, that I have mentioned earlier, will be put before you in brief in remedial suggestions by me, and I do hope that you will understand it.

IV

In India, since the year 1947 up to the year 2002, the amount of property that has been lost in communal riots, with that, if not more, at least 2 crores and fifty lacs people could easily be given employment; the problem of housing and education of the same number of people could be solved.

Due to the communal outbursts the occupational activities were affected, and that would be considered as national loss. With this loss the day-to-day problems of crores of people could be solved and their life could be made happier and more peaceful. But it is unfortunate that wealth and property, lost in riots, was burnt without any aim in a country like India in which crores of people are under poverty line. What should be done so that such situations are not faced? I once again appeal that if at all three levels-individual, community and government - something in a concrete manner is done stage by stage, the country would be free of communalism.

Let us, first of all, discuss the steps to be taken at individual level. India has a population of more than one hundred crores, in which 12 or 15 crores are Muslims. More than 80 crores are Hindus. It is possible that, due to differences with Hindus, such a large number of Muslims will disappear? Certainly not. Then, will they leave the country? It is also not possible. Most of the Muslims, more than 90 per cent of them, are Indians, i.e. they are born here. This country belongs to them too, and living here they have to build their future. There is no doubt about it. They have no other alternative other than this.

More than eighty crores Hindus cannot dream of a truly progressive India advance on the path of peace without co-operation of Muslims and other communities. It is only possible when all from majority and minority communities walk hand in hand.

Each and everyone have to make a balance between his or her own religious community and national interests, he or she has to unite with nationalism, and then should move forward. The teachings of a religious, community may be great, but the followers of the community concerned should understand that nationalism is greater. If they do not become familiar with this fact, they will be away from national stream; they will suffer. This fact relates not only to India but also to many other countries of the world.

Each and every religious community has been founded on the basis of certain values that were best and necessary for circumstances of the country and times. Goodness like adjustment with others, or co-operation, or consistency can be found in their teachings. But by not moving according to the teachings of their religious community those who depend upon fundamentalism and conservative practices, or those who use their co-religionists taking advantage of their poverty, illiteracy or innocence, are dishonest towards their own self, their co-religionists and also towards those great leaders who founded the religious community. Everyone must understand this fact also. Along with this, leaders of all communities, by knowing it, must come forward for an atmosphere surcharged with harmony, in which lies their welfare too.

Policies like appeasement, fun and frolic with the sentiments of people for individual and party interests, and selection of candidates on the basis of religious community or sect by keeping aside the qualifications, one, certainly, does the things against national interest or nationalism; are reflections of lower national thinking. That is why; these kinds of acts should be stopped at government level and also at the level of political parties.

There is a great need to work towards eradicating the problem of unemployment among the youths, illiteracy and poverty and that too with honesty and without any discrimination. This will help in solving many problems, and will create awakening. The result will be in checking on communalism to a great extent. That is why it is expected that a lot of work have to be done at government level in this direction.

Thus, in order to get rid of the problem of communalism in India, there is a need of collective efforts. All will have to discharge their duties. If we do so, definitely harmony will prevail. Everybody will prosper. This must be done; this was the dream of Mahatma Gandhi for a free India.

References:

1-2. About peace brigades and volunteer corps Mahatma Gandhi wrote in *Harijan* on 18-06-1938 and 05-05-1946 respectively. Extracts of his writings are being given in appendix C and D.

☐☐☐

APPENDICES

A. SELF-SUPPORTING EDUCATION

The suggestion has often been made ...that in order to make education compulsory, or even available to every boy and girl wishing to receive education, our schools and colleges should become almost, if not wholly, self supporting, not through donations or State aid or fees exacted from students, but through remunerative work done by the students themselves. This can only be done by making industrial training compulsory. Apart from the necessity which is daily being more and more recognized of students having an industrial training side by side with literary training, there is in this country the additional necessity of pursuing industrial training in order to make education directly self-supporting. This can only be done when our students begin to recognize the dignity of labour and when the convention is established of regarding ignorance of manual occupation a mark of disgrace. In America, which is the richest country in the world and where, therefore, perhaps there is the least need for making education self-supporting, it is the most useful thing for students to pay their way wholly or partially...If America has to model her schools and colleges so as to enable students to earn their scholastic expenses, how much more necessary it must be for our schools and colleges? Is it not far better that we find work for poor students than that we pauperize them by providing free studentship? It is impossible to exaggerate the harm we do to Indian youth by filling their minds with the false notion that it is ungentlemanly to labour with one's hand and feet for one's livelihood or schooling. The harm done is moral and material, indeed much more moral than material. A freeship lies and should lie like a load upon a conscientious lad's mind throughout his life. No one likes to be reminded in after life that he had to depend upon charity for his education. Contrarily where is the person who will not recall with pride those days if he had the good fortune to have had them when he worked in a carpentry-shop or the like for the sake of educating himself-mind, body and soul.

[Y. I., 02-08-1928]

B. RIGHTS OR DUTIES

I want to deal with one great evil that is afflicting society today. The capitalist and *Zamindar* talk of their rights, the labourer on the other hand of his, the prince of his divine right to rule, the ryot of his to resist it. If all simply insist on rights and no duties, there will be utter confusion and chaos.

If instead of insisting on rights everyone does his duty, there will immediately be the rule of order established among mankind. There is no such thing as the divine right of kings to rule and the humble duty of the ryot to pay respectful obedience to their masters. Whilst it is true that these hereditary inequalities must go as being injurious to the well-being of the society, the unabashed assertion of rights of the hitherto down-trodden millions is equally injurious, if not more the same well-being. The latter behaviour is probably calculated to injure the millions rather than the few claimants of divine rights. They could but die a brave or cowardly death but those few would not bring in the orderly life of blissful contentment. It is, therefore, necessary to understand the correlation of the rights and duties. I venture to suggest that rights that do not flow directly from duty well performed are not worth having. They will be usurpations, sooner discarded the better. A wretched parent who claim obedience from his children without first doing his duty towards them excites nothing but contempt. It is distortion of religious precepts for a dissolute husband to expect compliance in every respect from his dutiful wife. But the children who flout their parent who is ever ready to do his duty towards them would be considered ungrateful and would harm themselves more than their parent. The same can be said about husband and wife. If you apply this simple and universal rule to employers and labourers, landlords and tenants, the princes and their subjects or the Hindus and the Muslims, you will find that the happiest relations can be established in all walks of life without creating disturbances in and dislocation of life and business which you see in India as in other parts of the world. What I call the law of *Satyagraha* is to be reduced from an appreciation of duties and rights flowing therefrom.

What is duty of the Hindu towards his Muslim neighbour? His duty is to befriend him as man, to share his joys and sorrows and help him in distress. He will then have the right to expect similar treatment from his Muslim neighbour and will probably get the expected response. Supposing the Hindus are in a majority in a village with a sprinkling of Muslims in their midst, the duty of the majority towards the few Muslim neighbours is increased manifold, so much so that the few will not feel that their religion makes any difference in the behaviour of the Hindus towards them. The Hindus will then earn the right, not before, that the Muslim will be natural friends with them and times of danger both the communities will act as one man. But suppose that the few Muslims do not reciprocate the correct behaviour of the many Hindus and show fight in every action, it will be a sign of unmanliness. What is then the duty of the many Hindus? Certainly not to over power them by the brute strength of the many; that will be usurpation of an unearned right. Their duty will be to check their unmanly behaviour as they would that of their blood brothers. It is unnecessary for me to dilate further upon the illustration. I will close it by saying that the application will be exactly the same if the position is reversed. From what I have said it is easy enough to extend the application with profit to the whole of the present state, which has become baffling because people do not apply in practice the doctrine of deriving every right from a prior duty well performed.

The same rule applies to the princes and the ryots. The former's duty is to act as true servant of the people. They will rule not by right granted by some outside authority, never by the right of the sword. They will rule by right of service, or greater wisdom. They will then have the right to collect taxes voluntarily paid and expect certain services equally voluntarily rendered, not for themselves but for the sake of the people under their care. If they fail to perform this simple and primary duty, the ryots not only owe to return duty but the duty devolves on them of resisting the princely usurpation. It may be otherwise said that the ryots earn the right of resisting the usurpation or misrule. But the resistance will become a crime against man in terms of duty if it takes the form of murder, rapine and plunder. Force that performance of duty naturally generates is the non-violent and invincible force that *Satyagraha* brings into being.

C. PEACE BRIGADES

Some time ago, I suggested the formation of a Peace Brigade whose members would risk their lives in dealing with riots, especially communal. The idea was that this Brigade should substitute the police and even the military. This reads ambitious. The achievement may prove impossible. Yet, if the Congress is to succeed in its non-violent struggle, it must develop the power to deal peacefully with such situation. Let us therefore see what qualifications a member of the contemplated Peace Brigade should possess.

- He or she must have a living faith in *ahimsa*- the non-violence. This is impossible without a living faith in God. A non-violent man can do nothing save by the power and grace of God. Without it he won't have the courage to die without anger, without fear and without retaliation. Such courage comes from the belief that God sits in the hearts of all and that there should be no fear in the presence of God. The knowledge of the omnipresence of God also means respect for the lives of even those who may be called opponents or *goondas*. This contemplated intervention is a process of stilling the fury of man when the brute in him gets the mastery over him;
- The messenger of peace must have equal regard for all the principal religions on the earth. Thus, if he is a Hindu, he will respect the other faiths current in India. He must therefore possess a knowledge of the general principles of the different faiths professed in the country;
- Generally speaking this work of peace can only be done by local men in their own localities;
- The work can be done singly or in groups. Therefore no one needs wait for companions. Nevertheless one would naturally seek companions in one's own locality and from a local Brigade;

- This messenger of peace will cultivate through personal service contacts with the people in his locality or chosen circle, so that when he appears to deal with ugly situations, he does not descend upon the members of a riotous assembly as an utter stranger liable to be looked upon a suspect or an unwelcome visitor;
- Needless to say, a peace bringer must have a character beyond reproach and must be known for his strict impartiality;
- Generally there are previous warnings of coming storms. If these are known, the Peace Brigade will not wait till the conflagration breaks out but will try to handle the situation in anticipation;
- Whilst, if the movement spreads, it might be well if there are some whole-time workers, it is not absolutely necessary that there should be. The idea is to have as many good and true men and women as possible. These can be had only if volunteers are drawn from those who are engaged in various walks of life but have leisure enough to cultivate friendly relations with the people living in their circle and otherwise possess the qualifications required for a member of the Peace Brigade; and
- There should be a distinctive dress worn by the members of the contemplated Brigade so that in course of time they will be recognized without the slightest difficulty.

These are but general suggestions. Each centre can work out its own constitution on the basis here suggested.

D. VOLUNTEER CORPS

Ordinarily, the efficient running of a large volunteer corps based on force implies the philosophy of the use of force in the event of breach of discipline. In such bodies little or no stress is laid on a man's character. Physique is the chief factor. The contrary must obtain in non-violent bodies in which character or soul force must mean everything and physique must take second place. It is difficult to find many such persons. That is why non-violence corps must be small, if they are to be efficient. Such brigades may be scattered all over, there may be one each for a village or a *mohalla*. The members must know one another well. Each corps will select its own head. All the members will have the same status, but where everyone is doing the same work there must be one person under whose discipline all must come, or else the work will suffer. Where there are two or more brigades the leaders must consult among them selves and decide on a common life of action. In that way alone lays success. If non-violent volunteer corps is formed on the above lines, they can easily stop trouble. These corps will not require all the physical training given in *akhadas*, but a certain part of it will be necessary.

One thing, however, should be common to members of all such organizations and that is implicit faith in God. He is the only companion and doer. Without faith in Him these Peace Brigades will be lifeless. By whatever name one calls God, one must realize that one can only work through His strength. Such a man will never take another's life. He will allow himself if need be, to be killed and thereby live through his victory over death.

The mind of the man in whose life the realization of this law has become a living reality will not be bewildered in crisis. He will instinctively know the right way to act.

In spite, however, of what I have said above I would like to give some rules called from my own experience:

- A volunteer may not carry any weapons;
- The members of a corps must be easily recognizable;

- Every volunteer must carry bandages, scissors, needle and thread, surgical knife etc., for rendering first aid;
- He should know how to carry and remove the wounded;
- He should know how to put out fires, how to enter a fire area without getting burnt, how to climb heights for rescue work and descend safely with or without his charge;
- He should be well acquainted with all the residents of his locality. This is a service in itself; and
- He should recite *Ramanama* ceaselessly in his heart and persuade others who believe to do likewise.

Man often repeats the name of God parrot-wise and expects fruits from so doing. The true seeker must have that living faith which will not only dispel the untruth of parrot-wise repetition from within him but also from the hearts of others.

❑❑❑

"Mahatma Gandhi is another Christ".

–Romain Rolland

Glossary

Ahimsa	:	Non-violence
Akhada	:	A wrestling ground; arena; ring
Bharat Mata	:	Mother India
Bhoomi	:	Land; soil; region; country; place; site; Area; the earth, world
Gana	:	A group; troop; a republic
Ganesh	:	Lord of attendant; the god Ganesh
Goonda	:	A dissolute person; lout; bully
Harijan	:	Untouchable; an English weekly started by Mahatma Gandhi in forth decade of twentieth century
Harijan Sewak	:	A Hindi weekly started by Mahatma Gandhi in the fourth decade of twentieth century along with Harijan
Hindustani	:	A mixed Hindi dialect of the Delhi Region that came to be used as a lingua franca widely throughout India including Pakistan of the day

Karma	:	Action, deed
Mahatma	:	Great soul; a high-souled person; a title bestowed on M. K. Gandhi by Rabindra Nath Tagore
Mahotsav	:	A grand function
Mohalla	:	Locality; suburb; quarter [of a town]; ward
Nagri	:	The Devanagri script
Navjivan	:	New life; A weekly started by Mahatma Gandhi both in Hindi and Gujarati from Ahmedabad in 1919
Pooja	:	Worship; adoration; veneration; homage; idolatry
Ramanama	:	The name of Rama, the [unknowable] name of God
Ryot	:	Subject
Sardar	:	A leader
Sarvodaya	:	General rise or progress; a movement launched by Mahatma Gandhi aiming at the amelioration of life in all the fields
Satya	:	Truth; real; genuine; pure; ultimate reality
Varna	:	Colour; quality; class; one of the four divisions of Hindu society

Vedic	:	Related to Vedas-the most sacred and Ancient scriptures of Hindus-four in number
Yajna	:	Plan; planning; step; measure
Young India	:	An English weekly started by Mahatma Gandhi From Ahmedabad along with Navjivan in 1919
Zamindar	:	A landlord; landowner

□□□

WHO'S WHO ?

Alexander	:	*Russian Emperor in eighteenth-nineteenth century A.D.*
Anand, C. S.	:	*A peace worker and professor at the Department of political science, Thammasat University, Bangkok, Thailand*
Confucius	:	*A renowned Chinese Philosopher [551-479 B. C.]*
Göhler, G.	:	*A professor at Frie University, Berlin, Germany*
Kabila Singh, C.	:	*Former Directress of Indian Studies Centre at the Thammasat University, Bangkok, Thailand*
Lambert, R. C.	:	*An eminent and modern western Social Scientist*
Mashruwala, K. G.	:	*A well-known Gandhian thinker of twentieth century*
Marx, Karl	:	*A German philosopher and father of Scientific Socialism [1818-1883 A. D.]*
Napoleon, B.	:	*Dictator of France in eighteenth-nineteenth century A. D.*
Shivaji	:	*A great Maratha Sardar of 17th Century A.D.*
Socrates	:	*A great Greek Philosopher [469-399 B. C.]*
Zoroaster	:	*Propounder of Zoroastrianism or Parsee Faith*

INDEX

INDEX

□□□